COUNSELING THE OLDER ADULT

A Training Manual

for Paraprofessionals and Beginning Counselors

by PATRICIA ALPAUGH and MARGARET HANEY

Lexington Books
D.C. Heath and Company
Lexington, Massachusetts
Toronto

This monograph is published by the
Ethel Percy Andrus Gerontology Center
University of Southern California

RICHARD H. DAVIS, Ph.D.
Director of Publications and Media Projects

ISBN 0-88474-043-9

Library of Congress Catalog Card Number 77-99241

Managing Editor: Richard Bohen
Cover Artist: Jesus Perez

Dedication

This manual is dedicated in gratitude to the peer counselors of the USC Andrus Gerontology Center:

Muriel Brandstater

Julia Carpenter

Eleanor Cheny

Jack Donohue

Claire Flint

Sister Alma Rose Gaffney

Charles Grannis

Elizabeth Hummel

Ralph Hunter

Hallie Jonas

Rosa Jones

Frances Kuppin

Marie Lawson

Myrtle Little

Bill McCoard

Sister Kathryn Mulligan

Margaret Pick

Vilma Proctor

Judy Raffel

Hannah Rau

Rubye Runyan

Lilyan Russell

Elestia Shackelford

Allan Spotkov

Rowena Spotkov

Milton Tepper

Jeanne Wilson

Laura Winston

Frieda Zimmerman

Helen Zimnavoda

In Appreciation

The authors would like to thank Kathleen Larkin, M.Ed., and Robert Rosenblatt, M.Ed., for originating some of the exercises in this training manual and Frances Black, M.S.W., Marguerite Mullins, M.S.W., Margaret Reedy, Ph.D., and Janet Witkin, M.S., for their contributions to the text.

We want to express our appreciation to Mark Berger, Daniel Brandt, Jan Sappell, and Steven Zarit, Ph.D., for reading the manuscript for content and style.

We are grateful to Robert Haney, Luwanda Katzman, Ph.D., William Ofman, Ph.D., and Lisa Pomeroy, Ph.D., for their support and encouragement of our efforts.

Contents

Foreword

Communication skills affect those of all ages and yet little is written for the paraprofessional or counselor who works with the older adult. The situation seems to be changing for the better and this manual is a remarkable contribution to the field of counseling the older adult.

I know of no other manual on counseling skills for the older segment of our population that matches this one in clarity, cogency, and dependability of information. In my opinion, this work is the first successful attempt to produce a guide for counseling the older adult that does so with such scope, reliability, and sophistication.

The purpose of this manual is twofold: the teaching of basic communication and counseling skills; and the provision of basic information regarding the older adult. The information and skills which are presented in this work have been selected with care and the reader is clearly told the rationale and philosophy behind both these purposes. The material is presented in a fashion that should be readily comprehensible to the beginning as well as the seasoned professional. The authors have made their concepts totally understandable while maintaining a level of intellectual stimulation.

It's been my pleasure to work with Margaret Hickey and Patricia Alpaugh in teaching their skills to the older adult. It is out of their instructional endeavor that this manual has grown. The authors bring to this work uniquely broad and varied backgrounds which collectively include counseling psychology, clinical psychology, and gerontology.

The availability of this manual should greatly facilitate the teaching of counseling skills for the older adult and should provide an incentive for others to start such programs where none currently exist.

Kathleen M. Larkin, M.Ed.

Preface

It is nice to be able to welcome this publication since it is a very novel approach to a basic need, that of helping to train persons to work with older adults on mental health related issues. There has been almost a total absence of practical training materials for professionals, paraprofessionals, and peers to draw upon in their work with older adults. The mental health movement almost by-passed the mental health needs of older individuals. Why the mental health needs of the group have been so neglected is something we all should be concerned about if not a little ashamed of. But here is interest, promise, and a basis for action.

This manual is, I believe, a first of its kind. It can provide a basis for teaching; it gives fundamental information about the processes of aging; and it moreover presents the "how to do it" of basic counseling skills. If one were to doubt whether something else is needed to supplement generic counseling training in order to be effective with older adults, read this manual. One cannot play God with any group; why should we presume we can help the older adult without becoming informed, sensitive, and experienced.

The field of service to the aging is expanding. Older adults are having their expectations raised about services and will want high quality attention in all areas from geriatrics to housing. It may be that among these needs the psychological factors that counseling addresses are central in their influence on the quality of life. Indeed, our experience at the U.S.C. Adult Counseling Center demonstrates how important that need is. The authors of this manual recognized that a very crucial step could be taken toward providing quality services in this area through preparation of an effective training manual, and in my opinion they have succeeded with this book. I believe it has potential for wide use, and I must congratulate the writers who gave their time, thought, and feeling to this pioneering work.

James E. Birren, Ph.D.
Director, Andrus Gerontology Center

Introduction

The growing population of adults over the age of sixty-five compels us to be concerned with the life satisfaction and mental health of older adults. At present, helping professions are not prepared to tend to the multiple psychological problems which afflict some members of the senior population. This book is an attempt to provide a practical solution to this difficult problem. It is our assumption that both old and young adults can, with proper training and supervision, learn skills which will enable them to become competent paraprofessional counselors. Our belief stems from research and practice. The research which supports this contention is partially based upon the finding of Robert Carkhuff (1969) who reports that there is extensive evidence to indicate that lay persons can be trained to acquire at least a minimum level of what he calls the "core conditions." These three conditions are found at high levels in counselors whose clients showed positive personality and behavioral change. The core conditions are empathy, respect and genuineness. These conditions may be viewed as interpersonal skills and therefore can be learned and brought to higher and higher levels in an individual through training and practice. This book is an attempt to provide lay persons with conceptual and experiential components of the core conditions. The text is a step by step progression of understanding and practice which hopefully will culminate in many paraprofessionals having interpersonal skills through which they can aid and comfort a great number of senior citizens. A pilot study by Francoise Becker (1976) indicates that the training program which gave us the idea for a book such as this showed significant positive improvement on two of the three core conditions. Since that study, the training program has undergone two revisions and a large, full scale research project is at present attempting to ascertain the level of effectiveness of the revised program. The revised program is the Nine Step Counseling Model which is outlined in this text.

The belief in the effectiveness of peer and paraprofessional counseling also stems from our experiences with trained peer counselors now working at the USC Adult Counseling Center, as well as at some neighboring centers. We have found that the invaluable services performed by the Peer Counselors have stood the test of time and competency. The enthusiasm and energy of the Peer Counselors as well as their expressed feelings of satisfaction with their new careers adds another positive dimension and fortifies our confidence in the future of paraprofessionals in the area of mental health services to the elderly.

The psychological and philosophical view of man which permeates this book is one which is in accordance with the Carkhuff notions about effective counseling. We believe people are free and do, indeed, choose their own destinies. Each individual has within himself the capacity to grow and to change if he wishes to do so. We feel that the counselor's objectives are to help counselees see their situations as clearly as possible, to support and respect the counselees, and to re-affirm at all times the counselee's dignity as a free respectable human being. Therefore the primary goals of counseling for the client are increased self-awareness and acknowledgment of responsibility for one's own actions. It is for the implementation of these objectives that the program was created and developed.

1

The first five chapters have been designed to develop the core conditions of empathy, respect and genuineness and to teach active listening skills. The development and learning process involves short lecturettes followed by class exercises. The teaching style of these chapters and the rest of the manual is an experiential one in which complex learning tasks are divided into simple components that can be mastered through discovery and practice.

To reiterate, two main objectives of the counselor are to support the client and clarify problems and the issues involved in these problems. This training manual presents a counseling model in Chapters 6 through 9 which is a framework within which the counselor achieves these goals. The counseling model is not effective in and of itself. It must be used by a counselor who has developed the core qualities. By developing the qualities of empathy, respect and genuineness, the counselor is able to form the type of relationship which is instrumental in achieving our counseling goals. The following nine steps constitute the counseling model:

1. Understanding the client
2. Establishing rapport
3. Defining the problem
4. Setting a goal
5. Clarifying issues
6. Listing alternatives
7. Exploring alternatives
8. Reaching a conclusion
9. Providing closure

The Readings on Aging are an essential part of this manual. They summarize information pertinent to counseling the older adult and contradict some common false beliefs about the aging process. Accurate knowledge about the aging process is vital for counselors of older adults. It helps the counselor understand the physical, psychological, and environmental issues which help shape the older individual's world view. It increases accurate empathy. It demythologizes the counseling situation. Finally it makes it possible for the counselor to provide accurate information to the older client, information which might very well be crucial to their physical or psychological welfare.

It is our desire that you will find the training materials as effective as we have. For us, the training sessions have been both enjoyable and personally rewarding, and we hope your experience will be similar.

Hopefully, our joint efforts will begin to meet the tremendous need for paraprofessionals and professionals who can provide mental health services to the older population.

Attending to Feelings

Feelings play a very important part in any problem presented by a client. In everyday living, people tend to negate how they feel about a problematic situation and concentrate instead upon what seems rational. When the feelings are neglected, the problem is never seen clearly. The counseling session is a unique opportunity for the client and counselor to explore all aspects of a situation, including the feelings the client has about his/her problem. Before embarking on the task of learning to work with feelings in the counseling session, the counselor should be aware of some notions concerning feelings.

* Feelings are neither good nor bad; they just are.
* Everyone has a RIGHT to his/her feelings.
* Feelings ALWAYS make sense when considered in context of the individual's world view.
* Feelings are not dangerous. Actions can be dangerous.
* Denying a feeling does not make it go away.

A lack of appreciation for these dynamics of feelings can result in actions by the counselor in which she/he attempts to: a) negate the validity of the client's feelings, b) deny the existence or importance of his/her feelings, c) try to suppress the counselee's expression of feelings, d) imply there is something wrong with what the client is feeling. Such counselor behavior not only detracts from the efficiency of the counseling session, it also violates the client; that is, it relays a message that the client is somehow "not o.k."

EXERCISE ONE: DEVELOPING A FEELING VOCABULARY

The counselor who is familiar with a wide range of adjectives finds it easier to specify what the client is feeling. The following list of feeling words has been devised to aid the counselor in improving his/her feeling vocabulary. As you read the list, other feeling words will probably come to mind. If you think of any additional words, add them to the list. You may want to share them with the group.

A VOCABULARY FOR FEELINGS

abandoned
accepted
affectionate
afraid
alarmed
amazed
angry
annoyed
anxious
appreciative
apprehensive
approval
ashamed
balmy
belittled
belligerent
bitter
bored
bottled up
calm
capable
competent
confident
conflicted
confused
contented
crushed
defeated
depressed
desolate
desperate
despondent
discouraged
disinterested
disparate
dissatisfied
dispassionate
distressed
ecstatic
elated
embarrassed

empty
enthusiastic
envious
euphoric
excited
exhilerated
fearful
friendly
frustrated
furious
futile
grateful
guilty
happy
hateful
helpless
hopeless
horny
humble
humiliated
hurt
identification
inadequate
incompetent
inflamed
insecure
insignificant
jazzed
jealous
joyful
lonely
longing
loved
loving
miserable
misunderstood
needed
negative
neglected
nervous
numb
passionate
pleased

pressured
proud
put down
puzzled
reborn
regretful
rejected
rejecting
rejuvenated
relaxed
relieved
resentful
sad
satisfied
sensual
serene
sexy
shocked
startled
surprised
tearful
tense
terrified
threatened
thrilled
transcendent
trusting
uncertain
uncooperative
understood
uneasy
unhappy
unloved
upset
uptight
vengeful
vindictive
wanted
warmhearted
worthless
worthy
yearning

EXERCISE TWO: REMEMBERING FEELINGS

In order to understand what a client could be feeling in certain situations, it is important that the counselors be able to experience feelings at deeper levels themselves. This exercise is designed to aid the counselors in becoming aware of their own feelings.

1. Find a comfortable position and become as relaxed as possible.

2. Once you are relaxed, try to recall in vivid detail an event or experience that made you feel good. Take your time, concentrate on the details of the situation, and recapture as many pleasant feelings as you can that are associated with that event.

3. When the trainer calls time, look back to your vocabulary sheet and mark off the words which best describe your feelings.

4. After the group has discussed pleasant feeling words, relive an experience which was painful. When the trainer ends the exercise, mark off on the feeling sheet those words which best describe how you felt in that situation. You may wish to share some of the feelings you experienced with the group.

EXERCISE THREE: IDENTIFYING FEELINGS

It is sometimes possible to imagine how a client might be feeling from the content of his statements to you. The following exercise offers a typical series of clients' statements and is accompanied by words which could describe what the client is feeling.

1. Statement: "I don't know what to do, I'm just going to have to give up. Nothing I do is right."
    Feelings: resigned, futile, hopeless, depressed, discouraged, unhappy, frustrated, desperate.

2. Statement: "My daughter suddenly told me I could no longer live with her and her family. I just didn't know what to say, what to do."
    Feelings: surprised, confused, startled, rejected, hurt, angry, anxious, shocked.

3. Statement: "You seem to understand what I'm talking about. You have no idea how hard it is to get people to understand. This is really great."
    Feelings: understood, grateful, happy, accepted, relieved.

Read each of the following counselee statements. In the space marked "Feelings," describe how the client may be feeling. Refer to the Feeling Vocabulary List for more specific adjectives. Compare your answers with other group members. Do not place any answers in the space marked "Response."

1. Statement: "Things will never be the same. It's terrible. I feel like giving up."

   Feelings:

   Response:

2. Statement: "Right now I'm pretty alone. Deserted you might say. My wife is dead and I don't like to go out much. I watch T.V. some, but it really doesn't interest me that much."

   Feelings:

   Response:

3. Statement: "My daughter's going to be here for Christmas. It's been so long since I've seen her. She said she could even stay beyond the holidays."

   Feelings:

   Response:

4. Statement: "I never thought I'd feel that way about a son of mine. I've always been so proud of him. I loved him so much and did everything I could to raise him right. Now he goes out and does a thing like this."

   Feelings:

   Response:

5. Statement: "I don't trust my doctor. He says one thing to me and another to my children. I wish I didn't have to go back."

   Feelings:

   Response:

6. Statement: "I'd like to talk about it but I just can't. It's one of those things we were raised not to talk about. It's just too personal a thing to talk over with someone, especially a stranger."

   Feelings:

   Response:

Self-evaluation: After listening to the responses of the other group members, do you feel that you were able to be specific and identify feelings?

6

EXERCISE FOUR: RESPONDING TO FEELINGS

When you the counselor focus in on how the client feels, you are responding in a facilitative manner. In reflecting how the client is feeling you are doing one or more of the following:

1) showing the client that you understand some of what he is experiencing,
2) supporting his feelings and thus supporting him,
3) helping the client focus in on his feelings,
4) checking out your guesses as to how he may be feeling,
5) giving the client the implicit message that you accept his feelings.

Some examples of counselor statements which reflect feelings are listed below:

"If I were in that situation I might feel helpless and frustrated."
"You are feeling helpless and frustrated now."
"What she said hurt you deeply."
"You feel rejected and belittled."

Return to EXERCISE THREE and write a response to the client which reflects his feelings. Discuss your responses with the group.

EXERCISE FIVE: THE COUNSELOR AND HIS FEELINGS

The instrument you use in a counseling session is yourself. Just like the counselees, you bring all of who you are into the session, and this certainly includes all of what you feel. Read the following statements and discuss with the group leader and the group the meaning and implications of these statements.

* It is impossible for a counselor not to experience feelings during a session.
* Hiding strong feelings during a session can confuse the counselee, and sometimes even invalidate him.
* If a counselor has great difficulty accepting and validating his own feelings, then he will have difficulty accepting and validating his clients' feelings.

HOMEWORK

The following questions are ones which you will need to consider carefully. The questions are designed to help you understand yourself regarding your own experience and expression of feelings.

1. Which feelings make me uncomfortable when I experience them?

2. Which feelings do I tend to deny because I believe that I "shouldn't" be feeling them?

3. Which feelings, when expressed by others, make me uncomfortable?

4. Are some of my feelings frightening to me? Which?

5. Am I usually aware of when I am feeling angry, anxious, uncomfortable, inadequate or embarrassed?

6. Do I withhold showing my feelings most of the time?

SUGGESTED ANSWERS TO EXERCISES

EXERCISE THREE:

1. rejected, hopeless, depressed, desperate, defeated, longing, helpless, discouraged

2. bored, lonely, unhappy, rejected, unloved, miserable, let down

3. joyful, happy, grateful, lonely, anticipation, uncertain, uneasy

4. sick, frustrated, disgusted, unhappy, discouraged, anger

5. distrust, fear, anxiety, belittled

6. inhibited, reluctant, distrustful, mixed, embarrassment

READINGS ON AGING

There are many myths about older people — about how they learn, how they relate to others, and how they respond to counseling. In order for you to become an effective counselor for older adults, you need to know what is fact and what is fiction. To help you do this, there is a section in each chapter which presents the facts about a certain area in gerontology. Following the readings there are short quizzes to help you learn the material. The answers to each quiz are in the back of your manual.

READING 1
BEHAVIOR AND AGING

There are some behavior changes with advancing age. The most significant ones are easily observed, and descriptions of them can be found in literature written thousands of years ago. The Greeks described the slower pace of the older person, whose movements are sometimes limited by stiffening in the joints. These descriptions usually mention grey hair and dry skin, as well. This slowing with age is the most significant, best documented change that is seen in the behavior of older adults. They don't walk as quickly as young adults. An old man doesn't reply to questions as quickly as a young man does. In general, it takes older people a longer time to respond to an event or stimulus. For example, when a signal turns green, it will usually take longer for an older person to start to walk across the street. In psychological terms, an older person's slower response in different situations is called "increased reaction time."

Because an older person is slower to respond, his timing may not be as appropriate. The older person may respond too late. For example, by the time he responds to a "WALK" signal and begins to cross the street, the signal may already have changed to a flashing "DON'T WALK" sign.

Also, this slowing of behavior means it takes the older individual longer to complete a task. Because of this, he can complete fewer tasks than a younger person can in the same amount of time. As a result, the slowing of behavior limits the amount of activity in which the older individual can engage.

Growing old is not the only cause of slowness. When someone is depressed, they usually move slower and engage in fewer activities. When an older person becomes depressed, the slowing of behavior that comes with normal aging is exacerbated.

This slowing of behavior happens gradually across the adult life span. Because it happens gradually, most healthy older people develop ways of compensating for the slowing. Oftentimes, the older person adapts by avoiding situations with excessive time pressures. The young track runner who worked out to make his running time faster and faster may become a track coach in middle age and an advisor to younger coaches in old age. In this way, he progresses to jobs with less and less time pressure. Another way in which the older individual can adapt is to purposely limit his daily activities. The older professional may delegate many of his responsibilities to younger co-workers.

When most older individuals are forced into activities that have tight time pressures and/or too many activities, problems usually result. The older individual may become anxious when he/she realizes the gap between his/her ability to complete a task within a certain time at a certain level of competence and what is expected of him/her. Also, because that individual usually has less energy, he/she will probably become fatigued quickly. That individual may blame others for the pressured conditions and end up feeling resentful; or that individual may blame himself/herself for failing or not meeting the demands of the situation and become depressed.

QUIZ:

1. What is the major change in behavior with advancing age?

2. How can this change affect an older individual's life? Give examples.

3. What can make the effects of this change worse?

4. How can an older person compensate for this change?

READING 2
SENSATION AND PERCEPTION IN OLD AGE

In old age, sensory acuity usually declines due to injury, disease, or normal aging processes. However, there must be a major reduction in sensory acuity before it interferes with a person's ability to function adequately in the world. Usually, it is not until after age 70 that sensory processes impair behavior. When impairment occurs earlier, it is probably due to some other cause rather than normal aging. It is important to note how well your client has adapted to sensory losses.

In terms of an older person's ability to see, there is another change besides decreased acuity. Usually, it takes the older eye longer to adapt to darkness. So, when older individuals walk into a theater, they have to wait longer before they can see in the dim light.

Since older persons have poor sensitivity to light and greater sensitivity to glare, night driving can be difficult for them. In light of these changes in sight, certain conditions can make seeing and reading easier for them:

1. high illumination without glare;
2. short periods of exposure;
3. enlarged figures;
4. figures that contrast greatly with their background.

Hearing losses that come with normal aging usually affect certain types of sounds. Older adults have more difficulty hearing high tones. Usually, older men have more of a hearing loss than older women.

There are four types of taste: salty, bitter, sweet, and sour. There is some evidence that as men grow older they need more salt on their food before they taste it. After the late 50's, there are declines in sensitivity to all four types of taste. Yet, these changes usually aren't large enough to be noticeable until after age 70. This loss of taste sensitivity after 70 may be why some older people lose interest in eating.

There is also a decline in their sense of touch. This is not very noticeable on a person's hand. The change is greater on an older person's feet and legs, which probably has less effect on functioning. There are changes in one's sensitivity to pain, as well. There is a 20 percent difference in the sensitivity to pain between young and old men.

Because of these changes in sensation and perception, the older individual is slower to respond to most sources of stimulation.

QUIZ:

1. At what age do sensory processes usually begin to impair behavior?

2. Describe the hearing losses that come with normal aging.

3. What conditions can make reading easier for most older individuals?

4. What consulting advice would you give to a nutritionist in a Board and Care home?

Attending to Content and Feelings

2

In Chapter One you were asked to listen carefully for feelings underlying the client's statements to you. By carefully noting the feelings accompanying a client's statement it becomes easier to comprehend the full meaning of his/her message. But listening for feelings only gives you part of the counselee's message. It is also necessary to listen to the content. By content we are referring to a brief summary of the client's message. In other words, the content is the gist of the client's statement, his central message. When a counselor responds to the content he filters the extraneous information and focuses on what he perceives to be the main issue. The extraneous messages may be important and therefore should be attended to and possibly responded to at a later time. Extraneous messages will be dealt with in a subsequent chapter. For the present however, we will concentrate on the central message, the content.

There are several reasons why restating both content and feelings can be very effective in the counseling session. The first and perhaps most important reason is that the counselee will feel understood when the counselor accurately reflects his/her message. Secondly, by reflecting content, the counselor and client will be able to focus on the most central and pressing aspects of the client's problem. Finally, reflecting content and feelings gives the counselor the opportunity to check to see if she/he has understood the client's message accurately.

Summarizing the client's message and arriving at a statement which reflects the content is not as easy as one might imagine. It is a skill which requires some practice. The exercises in this chapter should be very helpful toward developing that skill.

EXERCISE ONE: IDENTIFYING CONTENT

The following example extracts the content from a typical client presentation of a problem:

"There are really so many problems and things to consider. If we move my mother-in-law, where do we move her to? If we leave her with us, then what about the situation with the kids? And then there's my husband. Harry would think we're abandoning her. I just don't know what to do about it."

Content: Client does not know where her mother-in-law should stay.
Content: Client is ambivalent about having mother-in-law stay at home or move out.

Both of the above extracts state the approximate CONTENT of the client's message. In the following exercise, read over the clients' statements and summarize the content of each statement. When you finish you may wish to discuss your answers with the group. Check the suggested answers at the end of the chapter to see if your answers approximate those answers. Do NOT fill in the spaces marked FEELINGS and RESPONSE at this time.

1. "My daughter and I had a fight last night over her and my grandchildren spending Thanksgiving with my son-in-law's folks instead of with her Dad and me. I was trying to understand but I couldn't. Why does she all of a sudden prefer them to us? I had to get off the phone right away so I wouldn't cry. It doesn't make sense that they would spend two holidays in a row with his parents."

   Content:

   Feelings:

   Response:

2. "My husband had some of his old friends over last night. They were laughing and telling old stories and having a really great time. I sort of kept out of the way by making the coffee and sandwiches. The couple of times I did try to say something, they didn't seem to hear me. I felt awful."

   Content:

   Feelings:

   Response:

3. "Before my husband died I was so busy taking care of him that I didn't realize what was happening. Now that he's gone, I have no one. All our friends were people he liked, and I have no desire to see them anymore. Maybe he was all I had. He always told me he'd never leave me . . . . and now he's gone."

   Content:

   Feelings:

   Response:

4. "Last night my son took away the keys to my car. How does he expect me to get around? He told me I didn't see well enough to drive anymore and said he was afraid I was going to have an accident. Just because I ran a red light or two. Hell! Everyone does that now and then. I don't think my driving is all that bad. Anyway he has no right to tell me what to do. Do I seem all that old to you? Next thing you know he'll be saying I'm senile."

   Content:

   Feelings:

   Response:

5. "My son told me he wouldn't visit me if Mr. Sheridan were there. He said Mr. Sheridan is making a fool of me because no young man would spend time with me unless he were after my money. When I told him that Mr. Sheridan and I loved each other, he said that I needed someone to take care of me because I was getting myself into an awful mess. He said it wasn't proper for a woman my age to have boyfriends. Imagine! Calling a 52 year old man too young!"

Content:

Feelings:

Response:

6. "I don't know if I can talk to you or anybody. It's so hard to talk about these things. I hope I can, well . . . uh . . . . oh, I don't know.

Content:

Feelings:

Response:

EXERCISE TWO: Return to Exercise One in this chapter. After each client statement, list feelings which the client may be experiencing.

EXERCISE THREE: FORMULATING CONTENT AND FEELING RESPONSES

In this exercise you will be asked to formulate a response which reflects the client's feelings as well as the content of his/her statements. The following are examples of this type of response.

"Your husband's family has said painful things to you. You feel very hurt about this."

"Your financial situation is extremely difficult right now. That is probably very distressing to you."

Return to Exercise One. After each client statement, formulate a response which reflects feeling and content. Discuss and compare your answers with your group after you have completed the exercise.

EXERCISE FOUR: PRACTICING FEELING AND CONTENT RESPONSES

The group divides itself into dyads. One member of the dyad is a client while the other member is a counselor. The client tells the counselor about some event or situation in his life which is personal and about which he feels strongly. The counselor responds by reflecting feelings and content. After about seven minutes the roles are reversed and the exercise is repeated. Once both members have had an opportunity to speak and respond all discuss their experiences as clients, and as counselors. Listed below are some questions which will serve as an outline for the discussion.

1. Do you feel your counselor accurately reflected the content of your statements to him?

2. Did your counselor reflect all of what you were feeling? Which feelings did he omit? Did he reflect some things you were not feeling? If so, which?

3. Discuss with your partner your experience as a new client.
    a. How does revealing personal information usually make you feel?
    b. Did you feel comfortable revealing personal information with your counselor? Why or why not?
    c. If you had an opportunity to discuss more personal material with your counselor, do you feel it would be safe? Why or why not?

The group may wish to meet together to discuss what has been learned from this exercise.

HOMEWORK EXERCISES

EXERCISE ONE: RESPONDING WITH CONTENT AND FEELINGS

Read each statement and summarize the content. List possible client feelings and then write a response reflecting feelings and content. Suggested answers for this exercise will be found at the end of the chapter.

1. "I don't know anymore. I'm just not as fast and as quick as I used to be. I can't stand the notion of having to write things down in order to remember them."

   Content:

   Feelings:

   Response:

2. "Taking care of her can be unbearable at times. There are times when I just feel like walking out and never returning. But then I can't you know, she was such a good wife to me all those years."

   Content:

   Feelings:

   Response:

3. "Without a job I feel useless. I really need to work, do something useful. But do what? I go round and round on this. I don't know what to do with myself!"

   Content:

   Feelings:

   Response:

4. "A lot you know! What am I doing here anyway? I only came here cause my wife nagged me into it."

   Content:

   Feelings:

   Response:

5. "For so long I thought the kids needed me, but now I know they haven't needed me in years. What do I do now? There's no meaning to my life."

   Content:

   Feelings:

   Response:

SUGGESTED ANSWERS FOR EXERCISES I AND II

1. Content: Daughter wants to spend Thanksgiving with her in-laws.

   Feelings: hurt, confused, abandoned, angry, lonely, apprehensive, jealous.

2. Content: Woman's husband and his friends were having fun but she was not enjoying herself. She was quiet and kept out of the way.

   Feelings: embarassed, inadequate, alone, rejected.

3. Content: Her husband is dead. She has no close friends.

   Feelings: empty, lost, hopeless, deserted, hurt, lonely, possibly hurt and angry.

4. Content: The man's son took away the keys to his car.

   Feelings: angry, confused, hurt, helpless, fearful, insulted, belittled.

5. Content: Her son disapproves of her boyfriend.

   Feelings: angry, insulted, belittled, misunderstood, resentful.

6. Content: Client wishes to talk about her problem but is unable to do so.

   Feelings: confused, nervous, apprehensive, anxious, possibly afraid and embarassed.

SUGGESTED ANSWERS FOR HOMEWORK EXERCISES

EXERCISE ONE:

1. Content: Client is functioning more slowly and has some memory problems.

   Feelings: anxious, annoyed, resentful, fearful, inadequate.

2. Content: Client is experiencing difficulty in caring for his wife. He is also ambivalent about caring for her.

   Feelings: angry, resentful, confused, guilty, hurting, fed-up.

3. Content: Client wishes to be working but does not know what he wants to do.

   Feelings: confused, depressed, frustrated, perhaps inadequate.

4. Content: Client does not have confidence in counselor or perhaps counseling.

   Feelings: angry, resentful, hopeless, disappointed, annoyed.

5. Content: Woman feels she has no function.

   Feelings: confused, lost, inadequate, hopeless, helpless, depressed.

READING 3
CAN OLD DOGS LEARN NEW TRICKS?

When was the last time you heard someone say, "You can't teach an old dog new tricks?" Well, developmental psychologists don't have much to say about how old dogs learn, but they have been carefully studying learning in the current generation of older adults. The most important fact that comes from all their research is that older individuals CAN learn.

One problem in studying learning is that we cannot look inside someone's head to see if the new information or skill has been learned. We must infer whether or not someone has learned something by the way in which the person applies that learning in a way that we can observe. This observable application of a person's knowledge is called "performance" by psychologists and what is INFERRED by this performance is actual learning. In laboratory situations, the PERFORMANCE on learning tasks is poorer for older adults. However, psychologists are still debating whether or not this means older people are less able to learn.

Even though this question is as yet unanswered, researchers have found methods and conditions which make learning easier and faster for older adults. The following are the optimal learning conditions for older adults:

1. A long time to study material that is to be learned.

2. Allowing the older adult a longer time to respond in situations which require the application of newly learned information and/or skills.

3. In training a skill, directing the method toward acquisition of appropriate use rather than toward remembering and reiterating the principle involved.

4. Give instructions rather than (or at least along with) demonstrations.

5. Placing older adults in a learning situation where complicated behaviors are broken down into smaller component skills and each of these simpler components is learned in such a way that larger and more elaborate problem-solving strategies can be formulated from them. Such procedures should be administered with a minimum of instruction and demonstration.

6. Giving enough clues to optimize the chance of getting the right answer the first time. This minimizes errors and requires less "unlearning."

Counseling can involve learning for the client. From this information on learning in older adults, you can see that older clients CAN benefit from counseling. It may possibly take them longer, but not necessarily.

QUIZ

1. Can older individuals learn new information and skills?

2. How does the PERFORMANCE of older adults on learning tasks compare to that of young adults?

3. How would you teach an older individual a new skill? Pick any skill you choose, and use the conditions which enhance learning in older adults.

READING 4
INTELLIGENCE AND AGING

I.Q. tests were first developed by Binet. He developed them for French schools to help identify students who would have particular trouble in school so they could be placed in special classes. Therefore, I.Q. tests were originally viewed as methods of predicting a student's performance in school. When psychologists began to use I.Q. tests to study adults, they argued over what the results of these tests meant. It is not relevant to predict the ability of most 40 year olds to perform in the classroom because few of them are going to school. Generally, psychologists began to consider I.Q. tests to be measures of a person's "intellectual capacity." As I relate to you the findings about the relationship of intelligence and age, keep in mind that most studies in this area use I.Q. tests. These tests are thought to be measures of intellectual competence, but they may actually only be good predictors of how someone will perform in a traditional classroom situation.

I will briefly present the findings of the latest developmental research on changes in intelligence with age. From young adulthood and through middle age, there is a maintenance of intellectual functioning. After a certain age, somewhere between 70 and 80, there is some intellectual decline due to normal aging. Older people perform best when they work with familiar information and/or materials in familiar ways. It is more difficult for the older individual to manipulate unfamiliar materials in familiar ways and to manipulate familiar materials in unfamiliar ways. Although there is some intellectual decline observed in old age, the amount of decline is usually not large enough to interfere with an older individual's ability to function adequately in the world.

On intelligence tests which involve speeded tasks, older individuals do not perform as well as younger ones. This may be due to a slowing in information processing with advancing age.

The intellectual decline that normally occurs in very old age is moderate and gradual. Whenever there is a marked decline in an individual's intellectual functioning, it is important to look for medical and/or psychological factors that can cause a rapid decline.

QUIZ:

1. What do I.Q. scores measure or predict?

2. During what part of the life-span is intelligence relatively stable?

3. What intellectual tasks are most difficult for older individuals?

4. What would you look for as possible causes of rapid intellectual decline?

Understanding Non-Verbal Communication 3

When communicating with someone we often concentrate solely on what he is telling us. We hear the words, and our responses usually attend to them. Often we are unaware that people communicate as much and sometimes more through their bodies. Non-verbal communication is body communication. This communication can be as obvious as someone hitting us, or as subtle as someone daydreaming while pretending to listen. The body is the repository for feelings. When feelings are denied or ignored, a person's health and physical functioning are affected. People can lie to themselves or others, but their bodies never lie. Therefore, the body is an invaluable tool for helping both counselor and client become aware of unexpressed feelings. The following exercises will aid the counselor in understanding various kinds of body communication.

EXERCISE ONE: BECOMING AWARE OF NON-VERBAL COMMUNICATIONS

The client's body communication may be an indication of how she/he is feeling about himself/herself, his/her counselor, his/her situation, or even about the session itself. The counselor should recognize the significance of the client's behavior and be able to integrate such non-verbal communication with other information he/she receives from his/her client. Since it is not possible to include every form of non-verbal communication in one short lesson, the following check list is merely a simple outline of some common non-verbal communication which may occur during a session.

Study the behavioral check list below. You may wish to add to the list after discussing some items with the class. One or more volunteers may impersonate a client who exhibits some of the behavior included below, while the rest of the class check off their evaluations. Discuss your evaluations.

A. How does the client sit?
   1.___ rigidly _____ relaxed _____ slouched
   2.___ near the counselor _____ at a normal distance _____ far away
   3.___ fairly upright _____ leaning forward _____ leaning backward
   4.___ moving constantly _____ moving appropriately _____ never moving
   5.___ looking at counselor _____ sometimes looking at counselor _____ never looking at counselor
   6.___ chair facing counselor _____ chair facing away from counselor

25

B. How does the client speak?
1.___ too quickly _____ at a normal pace _____ slowly _____ very slowly
2.___ very loudly_____ in a normal tone _____ softly _____ barely audibly
3.___ with excess emotion _____ with some emotion _____ with no emotion
4.___ with many gestures _____ with some gestures _____with no gestures
5.___ with high pitched tones _____ with appropriate intonation _____with no intonation
6.___ with appropriate affect _____ with inappropriate affect _____ with no affect
7.___ with fluency_____ with blocks or stammers _____ with no fluency

C. How does the client look?
1.___ nervous _____ tense _____alert _____ relaxed _____ passive
2.___ coloring intense_____ coloring normal _____ pale and wan
3.___ happy_____ normal _____ sad _____ teary
4.___ well dressed _____ normally dressed _____ disheveled
5.___ very overweight _____ normal weight _____ very thin
6.___ comfortable _____ slightly uptight _____ frightened
7.___ friendly_____ businesslike _____belligerent _____ meek

EXERCISE TWO: IDENTIFYING BEHAVIORAL CUES

While not all behavior represents the same feelings, many types of behavior may represent some of the feelings listed below. The following excerpts describe the behavior of a client sitting across from you. Read the description, and see if you can guess what the client may be feeling.

NON-VERBAL COMMUNICATION	POSSIBLE CLIENT FEELINGS
1. Client sits very straight and rigid in his chair. He does not look at you directly. His lips are tight and when he speaks it is in a high-pitched voice. He speaks very rapidly.	a. anxious b. happy c. relaxed d. shy
2. Client takes a comfortable position in a chair. Her facial muscles are relaxed and she looks directly at you. Her voice is loud enough for you to hear. She speaks at a rate which seems natural for her.	e. satisfied f. afraid g. angry h. embarrassed i. sad
3. Client taps his foot. He looks away from you often. He rises and paces during the session.	j. depressed k. tense l. defensive
4. Client sighs.	m. uncomfortable n. comfortable
5. Client looks sleepy, listless.	o. uptight p. scared
6. Client is slouched in a chair. He doesn't appear to hear much of what you say. He looks drawn and tired.	q. annoyed r. relieved

7. Client seems silly. He laughs at inappropriate times.

8. Client talks very softly, choosing words with extraordinary care. He avoids eye contact and says very little.

9. Client's face is tightly drawn and her lips are pursed together. She seems to be glaring at you. Her face is slightly flushed.

10. Client's eyes are teary.

11. Client misses quite a few sessions. The reasons he gives for missing sessions seems trivial. When he comes, he's late.

12. Client always arrives one hour before a session. There are no apparent transportation problems.

EXERCISE THREE: INTERPRETING NON-VERBAL COMMUNICATIONS

From the following client descriptions and statements, extract the content, and list possible client feelings inferred from both their statements and body-language.

1. Client is slouched in the chair and speaks in a very soft voice. She seems listless and shows little emotion. "I don't know really. Trying to keep busy does no good. I can't seem to get out of this slump I'm in. I don't accomplish anything."

   A. Content:

   B. Feelings inferred from statement:

   C. Feelings inferred from body-language:

2. Client talks at a rapid pace. He appears rigid and tense. His skin tone is quite red. He paces the room while he talks. "I can't get anything from that damned agency. I get pushed from one secretary to another. I get so furious I feel like smashing someone."

   A. Content:

   B. Feelings inferred from statement:

   C. Feelings inferred from body-language:

3. Client sits comfortably and speaks directly in a pleasant tone. She smiles often. "Well, I must say I'm quite relieved and more than a bit grateful. There was a time — as you well remember — when I thought this thing would never be over."

A. Content:

B. Feelings inferred from statement:

C. Feelings inferred from body-language:

EXERCISE FOUR: LEARNING CONGRUENCY

Sometimes verbal communication and body communication differ. When this occurs the counselor should be careful to recognize the lack of congruence between what is said and what is expressed behaviorally. In the following exercise decide which client statements are congruent with non-verbal communication and which are not. Write CONGRUENT or INCONGRUENT after each statement. You may wish to explain why you answered as you did.

1. A young woman smiles as she speaks. Her voice is quite loud and her manner is animated. "I believe for the first time that I have some control over what happens to me. That gives me a lot of freedom. Things still upset me, but at least I don't feel hopeless."

2. A man of about 75 leans forward in his chair. His voice gradually rises as he speaks. His face is slightly flushed and tense. "When I see people my age patronized and laughed at on television, I feel outraged. I just don't understand why television writers don't at least attempt to portray older persons more realistically."

3. A woman of about 40 sits back in her chair. Her voice is flat and she speaks softly. She avoids eye-contact with the counselor and appears to be uninterested in the conversation. She drums her fingers occasionally. "No, I really don't know how you can say that. Why should I be angry with you. I don't think you said anything particularly hurtful to me. After all, you've got your opinion and I've got mine."

4. A young girl misses sessions rather often for no apparent reason. During the session her attention wanders. "No really, I like to come here. It really helps me. Anyway, if I really didn't want to come my mother couldn't make me."

EXERCISE FIVE: PRACTICING CONGRUENCY

The group divides itself into dyads. One member is the Speaker and the other is the Listener. The Speaker tells the Listener about some current event in his or her life. After about five minutes the Listener stops the Speaker and describes various aspects of the Speaker's body communication. If the Listener is aware of any incongruence between the Speaker's body and verbal communication, the Listener explains this to the Speaker. The roles are then reversed and the exercise repeated. It will be helpful for the Listener to refer back to the check list while the Speaker is talking.

HOMEWORK EXERCISES

EXERCISE ONE:

This exercise is designed to familiarize you, the counselor, with some aspects of your own non-verbal communication. In the space provided after each item, describe what your physical appearance might be like under the following circumstances.

1. You are at a party where someone is talking incessantly. You find them boring and obtrusive but feel you cannot leave the scene.

2. You are spending an afternoon visiting a favorite friend in his/her house. You are sitting in the living room or den and enjoying yourself immensely.

3. You are in the presence of a very angry person. This person is yelling at you and blaming you for something. You feel his accusations are unjust. He will not listen to what you have to say.

4. Remember a time when you felt out of place, shy, or inadequate. Imagine yourself in that situation again.

5. What makes you tense? Imagine such a circumstance and re-live it.

EXERCISE TWO:

Explain how you express yourself non-verbally when you are:

a. preoccupied

b. angry

c. depressed

d. pleased

Understanding Counselor Responses

In Chapters One and Two attempts were made to understand a client by noting the content of his conversation along with the feelings underlying that content. Chapter Three attempted an understanding of a client by noting and interpreting his body-communications.

Knowing a client in the most complete way is the first goal of counseling. This means being familiar with his unique "world-view." A person's world-view includes how he feels about himself, others, and the various events which make up his life experience. The person's world-view also includes his belief system. What does he believe about himself and others? How does he believe the world is structured? What are his beliefs about morality, the laws of nature and human behavior? What are his attitudes and values?

All humans experience the same feelings, but what causes one to feel joy may be a source of sorrow to another. It is this aspect of human experience which creates the amazing plurality within the human race. It is because of this plurality that the counselor cannot presume to know how his client feels or believes until he has consulted the client himself.

The client's world view is his frame of reference by which he judges the world. Since each counselor has his own unique world-view getting to know another means, at times, "suspending judgment" and leaving oneself open for the possibility that a client may view life quite differently. As one author put it so beautifully, it means "walking in another man's moccasins." When the counselor is able to suspend his own frame of reference and become immersed in his client's, he is being empathic and respectful of that client. Understanding in a deep way how another thinks or feels does not mean that one agrees with it. It simply means that one understands and hopefully respects the other's point of view.

In the following chapters you will become acquainted with various counselor responses. These responses have several purposes, one of which is to aid you, the counselor, to know your client better by getting a sense of his world-view.

EXERCISE ONE: RATING RESPONSES

In this exercise attention is given to the quality of a response. A response which is considered to be a high quality response is one which is both helpful to the client and respectful of his/her world-view. A poor response neither helps the clients nor respects them. This exercise presents three quality level responses, Level I, Level II and Level III. Study the definitions of the three, and discuss them with the group and group leader. Once the various types of responses have been discussed, read the directions for Exercise I and complete the exercise.

COUNSELOR RESPONSES:

Level I Implies that the client is somehow "not OK." A counselor who gives a Level I response does one or more of the following:
    a. She/He does not respect the client's feelings.
    b. She/He implies the client should not be feeling what she/he is feeling.
    c. She/He puts the client down.
    d. She/He comes up with quick solutions or advice.
    e. She/He responds in a sarcastic, unfeeling manner.
    f. She/He tries to top the client's story.
    g. She/He shows little respect for the client's world-view.

Level II Is a response which shows respect for the client and his/her world view. A counselor who gives a Level II response does the following:
    a. She/He responds to the stated feeling or content in an accepting manner.
    b. His/Her verbal as well as non-verbal behavior is attentive to the client.

Level III Is a response which is not only respectful of the client, but also encompasses the client's world-view.
    a. Counselor responds to the stated feelings and notes the undercurrents implicit in the client's statements.
    b. Counselor emphasizes the intensity of the speaker's feelings by his/her tone of voice, gestures and words which accent feelings.
    c. Counselor responds to non-verbal cues from client.

DIRECTIONS FOR EXERCISE ONE:

Read the following client statements and the counselor's response. Label each response I, II or III.

1. Client: "I don't know. It seems now that Bill is gone there's just nothing to live for. We didn't have that many friends, and most of the ones we did have have passed on. I don't want to be dependent on my daughter. She's got to have a life of her own. I just don't know."

   Counselor Response:
       LEVEL _____ "Why don't you join a Senior Citizen's Club?"
       LEVEL _____ "You must be very lonely."
       LEVEL _____ "You are feeling a great deal of loss from your husband's death. It must be difficult for you to know what to do next."

2. Client: "I don't seem to want to go anywhere anymore. You see, I don't hear so well and it's embarrassing to keep asking people what they said to me. Besides, I'm not sure anymore about what's going on around me. But then, when I stay home and don't go out I get very depressed."

Counselor Response:

LEVEL _____ "You shouldn't feel that way. At least you can hear a little. You know, there are a lot of people who can't hear anything at all!"

LEVEL _____ "You're embarrassed about your hearing problem."

LEVEL _____ "It sounds as if you feel you can't win. If you go out to meet other people you're embarrassed, but if you stay home you get depressed. Sounds as if you feel like you're really in a bind."

3. Client: "It's really strange. I was always so busy I never had this kind of problem. But now, it's not that I don't have anything I could do. But there doesn't seem to be anything I really want to do that much. So I drink more than I should and my wife thinks I should talk to someone about my drinking."

Counselor Response:

LEVEL _____ "It seems you're bored and don't have anything you really want to do now."

LEVEL _____ "Well, for a start, you've got to stop drinking. That's not at all a good way to solve your problem."

LEVEL _____ "Now that you are no longer working you seem to be without direction. Do you feel there's a connection between that and you're drinking?"

4. Client: "He doesn't understand. There's not enough to do around the house anymore. Anyway, why keep the place up when the kids are gone? It would be different if my husband appreciated the things that I do. But he doesn't. He never really did. When I complain that I'm bored he just lectures me about how lucky I am that I don't have to go to work every day. Maybe he's right, but if I'm so lucky, how come I feel so rotten?"

Counselor Response:

LEVEL _____ "You feel misunderstood and unappreciated by your husband."

LEVEL _____ "Why don't you learn to cook some new dishes? That would give you something interesting to do and probably make your husband happy."

LEVEL _____ "Your life seems to be rather directionless now. In addition to that, your husband is not attending to what you are saying to him. It must be difficult to be in this situation."

5. Client: "He said, 'Hurry up! Hurry Up! You're getting slower and slower.' And he says that after me putting in all those years in the company. I was working there when he was still in britches."

Counselor Response:

LEVEL _____ "You're feeling quite put down by your supervisor's remark."

LEVEL _____ "It sounds as if you are feeling the insult of the supervisors remark and are unappreciated for all the good work you did for so many years."

LEVEL _____ "Have you thought of retiring?"

DIRECTIONS:

For the following client statements formulate what you believe to be Level I, II and III responses. You may find it helpful to find a partner and one of you play the part of the client while the other responds with the three various responses.

6. Client: "I called my daughter yesterday and she said that she would have to get off the phone because she had to go somewhere. Lately this happens a lot. She doesn't seem to have time for me anymore."

Counselor Response:

LEVEL I Response:

LEVEL II Response:

LEVEL III Response:

7. Client: "Well, it's a matter of not being able to get going in the morning, or for the rest of the day. My house is a mess and although I have always been a neat person, I just can't seem to get the energy to do anything. I don't know what's come over me. I feel awful about the way I'm behaving."

LEVEL III Response:

LEVEL II Response:

LEVEL I Response:

8. Client: "I love my wife. I always have. But since she's been so ill, life has become a tremendous strain. I'm ashamed to have to say this, but sometimes I feel so burdened that I wish I could just go away and leave her and all this trouble behind. I know it sounds heartless, but there are times I really feel this strongly."

Counselor Response:

LEVEL II Response:

LEVEL III Response:

LEVEL I Response:

Check your answers to questions one through five with the answers provided at the end of the chapter. Discuss with your partner or the group the answers you suggested for questions six, seven and eight.

EXERCISE TWO: LEARNING TYPES OF COUNSELOR RESPONSES

Listed below are several modes of counselor responses. Since your goal as a counselor is to gain further insights into your client's world-view, while defining and clarifying his/her problem, these counselor responses are the means by which you can attain your goal. Read each response carefully and thoughtfully. Discuss the meaning of each response with your leader and your group.

COUNSELOR RESPONSES

Restating Content: Repeating the client's words or content. The purpose of this response is to clarify the issue for the counselor and/or client. Sometimes the counselor may wish to restate content to underline the importance of what the client has said.

Probing: Asking the client for further information for the sake of clarification or to obtain more pertinent details. The counselor may also wish to use a question as a means of helping the client focus on some important aspect of his/her situation. Questions should not be asked merely to fill in a space because the counselor does not know what to say. Also, they should not be used in a way which guides the client to a conclusion already arrived at by the counselor, as in the judiciary sense of "leading the witness."

Confronting: Pointing out either verbal or behavioral discrepancies which the counselor notes during the session. An example of this would be the counselor drawing the client's attention to his/her denial of anger in his statements, while his/her non-verbal communications are those of intense anger.

Reflecting Feelings: The counselor reflects both spoken and unspoken feelings which the client is experiencing. By reflecting feelings the counselor is being both empathic and supportive of the client.

Self-Disclosing: The counselor shares with the client his/her own experiences and feelings. Sometimes those experiences and feelings are directly concerned with the client. At other times they have to do with the counselor's life apart from the counseling session. These responses should be for the purpose of empathy or support for the client. At times they are a means of confronting the client.

Information Giving: If the client has a false belief about his/her situation, as in the case of the client who believes that impotency is an automatic consequence of old age, then the counselor shares his/her knowledge about sex and aging with the client.

Summarizing: The counselor brings together in an organized manner all that has been discussed about a particular issue. Sometimes the counselor may wish to summarize what has been accomplished in a session.

Interpreting: The counselor interprets when she/he makes inferences concerning the client or a particular issue under discussion.

Silence: A counselor may wish to remain silent when she/he perceives that the client has a need to "ventilate" or "dump." By ventilate and dump we are referring to the instance where a client has pent up complaints that she/he needs to release. Silence by both counselor and client can also be helpful for giving both a chance to absorb and make some sense of what has been discussed in the session. Sometimes a prolonged silence indicates that both client and counselor are "stuck," that is, neither knows how to continue the session. Being "stuck" can be very productive in a session. Together the counselor and client can examine how and why this situation came about.

EXERCISE THREE: IDENTIFYING RESPONSES

Two members of the group volunteer to play the counselor and the client. As they read from the script the rest of the group follows the script and identifies the type of response the counselor makes when she/he addresses the client. The members playing the parts may wish to go over the script alone before presenting it to the group. Once the script has been acted, the group checks its answers with those listed at the end of the chapter.

SCRIPT

(This is an excerpt from an actual counseling session. The client and the counselor have already had a session and therefore the initial introductions and statement of the problem are not included.)

Client	Counselor
"I was upset when I left you last week. You didn't seem to catch what I was trying to tell you."	
	1. "You felt misunderstood by me."
	RESPONSE: Reflecting feelings.
"Yes, quite. You implied that I was angry with my husband. Sometimes I get annoyed, of course, but I'm really not angry. No, I'm never angry at him."	
	2. "It was my feeling that sometimes you are quite angry. When you speak of your problems with him you often seem upset, even hostile."
	RESPONSE: _____

35

"Well I might SOUND angry, but really I love him very much."

"I've never thought of it that way. I've always tried to be a nice person. In my family being angry is frowned upon. It's the same as being out of control. It's just not allowed."

3. "It is possible to love someone and still be angry with them you know."
RESPONSE: _____

4. "If those are the standards you try to follow then you must experience a lot of conflict. Caring for a very sick and sometimes cranky husband would make anyone angry at times. Yet you don't seem to be able to experience anger without experiencing guilt also."

RESPONSE: _____

(Client begins to cry.)

5. (Counselor moves slightly forward, hands the client a kleenex.)

RESPONSE: _____

(After a while.)
"I'm really sorry. I don't have these outbreaks very often. You must really think I'm strange."

6. "No, far from it. I feel you have many reasons to cry. I cry at times myself, you know."

RESPONSE: _____

"Well, that's good to hear."

7. "Just exactly what made you cry?"

RESPONSE: _____

"It was what you said about feeling conflicted. You were very accurate about that. The truth is, sometimes I'd like to blow up or just leave. He's been bedridden for seven years and God knows how long this will go on. I do love him, but I just can't have a life of my own until this whole thing is over."

8. "You're feeling hopeless, aren't you?"

   RESPONSE:_____

"Yes, very. Hopeless and frustrated. My friend, Mary, says I take my responsibilities too seriously. She thinks I should get out and enjoy myself. But I can't seem to do that."

9. "You would feel too guilty."

   RESPONSE:_____

(Client nods her head affirmatively.)

10. "As I see it, you are in a difficult situation and because you feel guilty you can neither become angry or take time out. Would you say that is accurate?"

    RESPONSE:_____

"Yes, unfortunately it's quite accurate."

HOMEWORK

EXERCISE ONE: Fill in the blanks with the correct response.

1. A response in which a counselor divulges something personal about himself is called _____ .

2. A response which is essentially a question is called _____ .

3. A response which points out verbal discrepancies is called _____ .

4. A response which utilizes inferences is called _____ .

5. A response in which the counselor states how a client may be feeling is called _____ .

EXERCISE TWO: Label the following responses as Level One, Level Two or Level Three responses.

1. "Now you shouldn't cry. Things are sure to get better." _____ .

2. "You seem quite discouraged." _____

3. "Listen, I've been through that and much more. Courage!" _____

4. "From all that you've said I get the feeling that you've made up your mind to take some steps to relate to your mother differently." _____

5. "You don't want to be around him anymore." _____

EXERCISE THREE: (a) Respond to client. (b) Label the type of response you made. (c) State why you chose to respond as you did.

"I know I haven't got long to live. I guess I've become used to the idea. It's my wife I'm worried about. She has always depended on me, maybe too much. I can't imagine her getting on without me. She's so upset about this that I'm becoming extremely nervous myself."

1. Response:

2. Type:

3. Rationale:

SUGGESTED ANSWERS TO EXERCISES

EXERCISE ONE:

1. Level one
   Level two
   Level three

2. Level one
   Level two
   Level three

3. Level two
   Level one
   Level three

4. Level two
   Level one
   Level three

5. Level two
   Level three
   Level one

EXERCISE THREE:

1. Reflecting feelings
2. Confronting
3. Information giving
4. Interpreting
5. Silence
6. Self-disclosing
7. Probing
8. Reflecting feelings
9. Interpreting
10. Summarizing

HOMEWORK EXERCISES

EXERCISE ONE:

1. Self-disclosing
2. Probing
3. Confronting
4. Interpreting
5. Reflecting feelings

EXERCISE TWO:

1. Level one
2. Level two
3. Level one
4. Level two
5. Level two

READING 5
MEMORY

There are many older individuals whose mental capacities remain at a normal level. The belief that all older people have poor memories is a myth. However, some older individuals whose mental capacities are intact may have benign senescent forgetfulness but NOT organic brain syndrome. There are two kinds of forgetfulness that may occur in old age. They are the following:

1. BENIGN FORGETFULNESS: where the individual forgets the details of an event but not the event itself.

2. MALIGNANT FORGETFULNESS: where the individual forgets the recent events.

When the last type, malignant forgetfulness occurs, individuals may make up events to fill in the gap of forgotten events. They may also become disoriented and confused. Malignant memory dysfunction is a symptom of brain disease.

Sometimes an older person forgets recent events because these memories are painful. It may make the individual happier to dwell on past memories which are either more pleasant or which the person has idealized. Also, memory problems may be caused by emotional stress and preoccupation with problems.

When older persons are depressed, they, or their families, are more likely to complain that their memory is poor. Although memory complaints increase with depression, there is usually no real decline in the person's ability to remember. Neither depression nor age necessarily cause a memory deficit.

For a long time, scientists have been searching for a drug which will help memory problems. So far, they have failed. There is no drug that is effective in enhancing memory. On the other hand, there are some drugs which interfere with cognitive functioning.

"Senility" is a word which is sometimes casually applied to all older individuals, and it implies a poor memory. The word "senility" came from the medical term "senile dementia," which refers to brain dysfunction and disease and NOT to normal aging. SENILITY refers to a disease process; senescence is normal aging.

QUIZ:

1. What is the difference between "senility" and "senescence?"

2. What is the difference between BENIGN FORGETFULNESS and MALIGNANT FORGETFULNESS?

3. Why might an older individual forget recent events?

4. How does depression affect memory?

5. Are there any "memory pills?"

READING 6
ORGANIC BRAIN SYNDROME

Organic brain syndrome is found more often in older adults than in young or middle-aged adults. The symptoms of brain syndrome are usually described as follows:

1. disturbance and impairment of memory;

2. impairment of intellectual functioning or comprehension;

3. impairment of judgment;

4. disorientation;

5. shallow or labile affect.

The type of memory disturbance which is a symptom of organic brain syndrome is the malignant type described earlier. It usually involves forgetting such normally accessible information as the person's birth date, age, and the current date. The type of intellectual impairment which is a sign of brain syndrome usually includes the inability to do simple calculations and to recall simple bits of general information.

SHALLOW affect and LABILE affect are psychological terms which refer to a person's emotional state. A person with shallow affect does not show much emotion. In situations which normally bring joy or provoke anger, such a person may not respond at all. A person with labile affect may have extreme, very changeable emotional outbursts. A minor frustration may bring an outburst of anger, sobbing, or giddy laughter.

Impaired judgment and disorientation can indicate many things besides organic brain syndrome. When they occur in brain syndrome, they are usually severe. A normal older person may be disoriented when he moves into a new neighborhood; confusion and disorientation under such conditions do NOT indicate brain syndrome.

Brain syndrome may be either chronic or acute. CHRONIC brain syndrome refers to clinical cases where brain dysfunction is irreversible with the present state of medical and psychological knowledge. ACUTE brain syndrome refers to cases where the symptoms are reversible. Chronic brain syndrome may be mild, moderate, or severe.

Depression or other emotional problems can be confused with brain syndrome. The following are symptoms of emotional problems which sometimes lead to a MISdiagnosis of brain syndrome:

1. poor attention;

2. poor concentration;

3. preoccupation with somatic symptoms;

4. hypochondriasis;

5. fear of death;

6. feeling depressed, lonely, bored, or rejected;

7. anger directed at themselves, their children, or the world;

8. anxiety

Brain syndrome can be more accurately diagnosed through assessment techniques.

The causes of CHRONIC brain syndrome are being studied. In some cases, vascular problems may contribute to it. It may also involve a brain disease which causes the death of brain cells or tangles the connections between these cells. It may involve a virus, a genetic defect, and may be influenced by level of education.

ACUTE brain syndrome may be caused by malnutrition, infection, and inappropriate medication. The symptoms of acute brain syndrome which distinguish it from chronic brain syndrome are: 1) its sudden onset whereas CBS may occur gradually over a five year period; and, 2) the person's denial of symptoms, sometimes accompanied with delusions.

QUIZ:

1. What are the symptoms of organic brain dysfunction?

2. What type of intellectual impairment is a sign of organic brain syndrome?

3. What emotional problems can be confused with brain syndrome?

4. Why is it important to distinguish between acute and chronic brain syndrome?

5. What can cause acute brain syndrome?

6. Give an example of a case where disorientation is NOT an indication of brain syndrome.

Responding to Your Client **5**

In the first four chapters we mentioned that your first goal as a Counselor is to get to know your client as well as possible. In those chapters you learned how to get a sense of who your client is by understanding the content of his/her communications, his/her feelings, his/her non-verbal communications and appreciating his/her world-view. Another way to know more about your client is to be aware of certain "themes" which appear in his/her conversations with you. A theme song as defined by Webster is "a melody that so often recurs in a musical drama as to characterize it or part of it." The definition is an excellent analogy for what we are talking about when we speak of themes in counseling. A theme in a counseling situation is an idea, feeling, attitude or belief which so often recurs in the sessions that the counselor can infer that the theme is an integral part of the client's world-view. For example, a client who constantly interjects the notion that she/he can never get what she/he wants from life, is expressing a sense of helplessness. Because the client expresses this often, the counselor can then infer that the theme of helplessness is a component of the client's world view.

In Exercise Two of this chapter, you will learn how to make interpretations. Understanding the notion of "themes" will be a great help when attempting to formulate interpretations.

EXERCISE ONE: PRACTICING SELF-DISCLOSURE

In Chapter Four you learned that Self-Disclosure meant sharing one's personal experiences and feelings. Self-Disclosure is, therefore, a PERSONAL COMMUNICATION. Most of the communication that takes place in a counseling session is Personal Communication. IMPERSONAL COMMUNICATION on the other hand resembles a social conversation. Impersonal Communication is conversation which gives information about events involved in the life of the person speaking, but does NOT give information about any deep personal or emotional reactions to those events. In the following example, a woman relates an event which occurred the previous year. Her first communication is an example of Impersonal Communication. Her second communication is an example of Personal Communication.

> IMPERSONAL COMMUNICATION: "Last year my husband took sick rather quickly. Three days later he died. It was a shock for the whole family. He'd always been so healthy. It was so unexpected."

PERSONAL COMMUNICATION: "Last year my husband took sick rather suddenly. He died three days later. It was a terrible shock to me and for awhile I thought I'd never get through it. I can't remember ever having been so distraught. I feel stronger now, but when I think of it, even yet, I get very upset."

The following exercise is designed to familiarize you with the difference between Self-Disclosure, that is Personal Communication, and Impersonal Communication. The group divides itself into dyads. For five minutes one member discusses an event in his life. His discussion should be Impersonal. After five minutes he then discusses the same event in a Personal manner. When he is finished, the other member of the dyad does the sharing, first on an impersonal level, then on a personal level. When all group members have completed the exercise, the entire group discusses the exercise, using the questions below as a guideline.

1. How did you feel while self-disclosing?

2. How did you feel while your partner was self-disclosing?

3. What did you learn about your partner that you did not already know before the exercise began?

4. How do you feel about your partner now that he has shared some of his feelings with you?

5. How can a counselor's self-disclosure be helpful to a client? How will it affect the counseling relationship?

EXERCISE TWO: LEARNING HOW TO MAKE INTERPRETATIONS

As clients talk to their counselors over a period of time, counselors tend to gather information and make certain assumptions about the dynamics which motivate the client. When a counselor does this, she/he is making an INFERENCE about the client. In Exercise Three in the last chapter the counselor inferred that the client was feeling guilty. Certain clues found in the client's statements, expressions and feelings implied a sense of guilt. When the counselor shared his inference with the client, he was INTERPRETING.

Interpretations should be made after enough information has been given to warrant them. False interpretations, however, are always possible. You can minimize errors in interpretation by occasionally checking their accuracy with your client.

HOW INTERPRETATIONS ARE MADE

The counselor is aware of certain behaviors, words and content which seem to tie together and form a theme.

From the behaviors, words and content the counselor makes an inference about the client.

When the counselor tells his client what he has inferred, the counselor is interpreting.

EXAMPLE A:

Mrs. S. is a sixty-two year old woman who has come to see a counselor concerning a problem she is having with her forty-one year old daughter. Her daughter has moved in with her and according to the client, the daughter lost her job and has not looked for other employment. The client is afraid that her daughter will use up the few funds available and that the result will be disastrous for herself. She also tells the counselor that the daughter has many unpleasant habits which make living with her very anxiety provoking. The counselor also learns from the client that years ago, when the daughter was a child, the client was a severe alcoholic and had mistreated the daughter. When the counselor asks why she doesn't make certain demands that the daughter stop spending her money, the mother demurs, saying that she does not want to hurt the daughter.

INFERENCE: From the information given, the counselor has a hunch that the woman feels guilty about having mistreated her daughter as a child. Therefore she does not feel comfortable making demands of her in the present situation.

COUNSELOR INTERPRETATION: "I wonder if the fact that you treated your daughter badly when she was a child is stopping you from confronting her with her behavior now?"

CLUES: The client abused her daughter in the past. She does not want to "hurt" her at the present time.

EXAMPLE B:

Mr. A. says to the counselor: "Well I'm really getting worried about my forgetting. I'm getting on you know, just passed sixty-seven and you know what THAT could mean."

INFERENCE: The client is worried about approaching an age where he may become senile.

COUNSELOR INTERPRETATION: "You are worried that your forgetting may be a sign that you are getting senile."

CLUES: "I'm getting on" "just past sixty-seven" "worried about forgetting" "what THAT could mean."

DIRECTIONS FOR EXERCISE TWO:

Read the client statements below and from those statements make an inference about the client. Formulate an interpretation response and then list the clues from which you made your interpretation. It will be very helpful for you to discuss your answers with the group. Suggested answers to this exercise will be found at the end of the chapter.

1. Client: "I'm rather nervous around a lot of people. Especially at gatherings. The kinds of people I meet when I go to events with my sister are, well you know, very educated types. It's hard for me to think of what to say to them. They are such successful people. And so smart!"

47

Inference:

Counselor Interpretation:

Clues:

2. Client: "So you'll be gone for a couple of weeks. I SUPPOSE I feel all right about that, even though you ARE the only one I can talk with."

Inference:

Counselor Interpretation:

Clues:

3. Client: "You're right about that, I am lonely all right. But I don't want to hang around old people. No I won't join their organizations. That will just depress me. I may be seventy-six, but I intend to stay young as long as I can!"

Inference:

Counselor Interpretation:

Clues:

4. Client: "I don't know what you people do. My daughter said that I should come and talk to you about this thing. But I want you to know right off, I'm not crazy or anything like that. I know people who are battier than a deserted church tower. I just want you to get it straight that I'm right in the head."

Inference:

Counselor Interpretation:

Clues:

5. Client: "I just don't feel right about my mother going anywhere. People who love their mothers don't put them away. After all, you only have one mother and you should love and care for her while she's alive."

Inference:

Counselor Interpretation:

Clues:

EXERCISE THREE: FORMULATING A RESPONSE

There is no one correct response to any client statement. Responses tend to flow naturally from what the client is saying or from what is happening in the session. Counselor responses have been listed in an orderly manner in this manual. In real life however, responses are not always as organized and predictable. If the session is generally focused around the important issues involved in the problem, and if there is empathy and respect for the client, the counselor should feel free to respond naturally at his own pace and in accordance with his own style. While learning to formulate certain responses, however, it will be very helpful if the beginning counselor asks himself the following questions: What are my goals at the moment? Which do I wish to respond to at present: content? feelings? non-verbal communications? my reactions to the client? my feelings about the session? my client's world view? This exercise is an excellent opportunity to practice carefully thought-out responses.

DIRECTIONS FOR EXERCISE THREE:

The group leader or a member of the group reads client statements out-loud. The members of the group write their responses and under the heading marked "Rationale," give reasons for having given that particular response. For questions six through ten, different members of the group volunteer responses without writing them before hand. After each of the ten responses, the class discusses and critiques it.

1. Client: "You know, I'm so sick and tired of taking pills. I have a pill for this and a pill for that. I even have a pill to counteract another pill. I'd really love to flush them all down the toilet. I'm so sick of the whole business."

   Response:

   Rationale:

2. Client: "There is nobody left who even knows me, let alone cares for me. The truth is I could die tonight and no one would know the difference."

   Response:

   Rationale:

3. Client: "I don't know . . . uh . . . well, it's hard to . . . uh . . . oh, never mind.

   Response:

   Rationale:

4. Client: "I don't exactly know how to tell you this, but my husband, he never touches me. He reads those "girly" magazines all the time. Lord, you'd think that touching a real live woman would be better than looking at pictures all the time."

Response:

Rationale:

5. Client: "My daughter doesn't care. She never cared for anyone but herself. I spoiled her I did. I only thought of her all these years. And now that I'm old and she should be looking after me and taking care of me, she gets herself a new job and moves away!"

Response:

Rationale:

6. Client: "It's been this way for about the last eight months. When I touch her she doesn't respond the way she used to. When I make amorous moves she makes excuses and manages to change the subject. I don't know what's wrong with me. She was always very attracted to me in the past."

Response:

7. Client: "I'm forgetting more and more. You know, I can remember my Dad doing this a lot just before he became senile."

Response:

8. Client: "I'm terrified to leave my house. Even during the day. My neighborhood used to be such a nice place to live. But I've got to shop, and I've got to go to the doctor's. See, I get this rash every time, just before I leave the house. Those kids could easily kill me. They attack old people like me all the time."

Response:

9. Client: "I know he's dying and I should be more patient, especially now. But it's hard to not blow up at times."

Response:

10. Client: "I don't know what's wrong between us. When I came home last night, she turned the radio off without saying goodnight and went up to bed. She didn't even cook my supper. Not even that!"

Response:

EXERCISE FOUR: A PRACTICE IN RESPONDING

The group leader or a group member role-plays a client with a problem. The entire group will play the counselor. This is done by placing an empty chair across from the client. One member of the group volunteers to be the counselor and sits in the chair. He responds to the client until another group member stands behind his chair. This is a signal that the other member wishes to play the part of the counselor. When the person in the chair finishes his last response, he gives the chair to the new counselor. This continues until several members have had a chance to play the part of the counselor. While the client and counselors are speaking, the rest of the group critiques the session by noting the types of responses made by the various counselors. After the session is completed, the group discusses what went on in the session, and both client and counselors relate how they experienced the session.

HOMEWORK EXERCISES

EXERCISE ONE: USING CONFRONTATION

The counselor may wish to confront his client when one of the following situations arise:

1) the client's verbalizations contradict one another;
2) what the client is saying is not congruent with his non-verbal communications;
3) the counselor is experiencing negative feelings about the client or the session;
4) the counselor wishes to draw attention to something the client is doing that the counselor finds unpleasant, annoying or destructive to their relationship.

Confrontation can be done in such a way that the client receives necessary feedback and at the same time feels he has the counselor's acceptance and respect. This is accomplished more easily if the counselor uses "I" statements when formulating a confrontational response. Knowing WHEN to begin confronting a client is important. Many excellent counselors use confrontational responses in the very first session and find the results rewarding. They have a way of establishing rapport quickly and the counselee has a sense that the counselor is empathic and respectful of him. Other counselors use confrontational responses in later sessions and use the beginning sessions to establish a solid rapport with the client. Both ways are very effective.

The following examples demonstrate a counselor using confrontational statements:

"You have been telling me for some time how upset you are, but you come across cold and emotionless. It is hard for me to get a real sense of your distress."

"Everytime we begin to discuss your feelings you change the subject. I would like to know why you do that."

"You say you are lonely and want friends. But when I try to befriend you and communicate with you, you say sarcastic things to me and then withdraw. I find it very hard to be a friend to you."

"I am becoming annoyed with you now. I feel you are blaming and attacking me. What am I doing that is making you so angry?"

DIRECTIONS FOR EXERCISE ONE:

Because confronting your client may be the most difficult thing you will have to do as a counselor, you should take some time to consider how you feel about confrontation. The following questions can be used as a guideline for thinking about this important issue. If confrontation raises some problems for you, as it does for a great many people, you may wish to discuss the issue with the group leader.

1. Are you generally able to tell people what you truly think about them when it is necessary or advisable?

2. Do you fear people will like you less if you give them negative feedback?

3. Do you believe people will "fall apart" if you tell them something about themselves which they find painful to hear?

4. Read out loud the confrontational statements in the introduction to this exercise. Imagine you are saying them to a client. What are you feeling as you say them?

5. How are you feeling while someone is telling you something you don't like to hear about yourself? How do you feel about it after some time has passed?

6. Can you think of a person who has told you something negative about yourself and although you were hurt, you nevertheless felt loved and respected by that person? If you can think of such a person, consider what it is he or she does that makes confrontation a constructive experience.

SUGGESTED ANSWERS TO EXERCISES

EXERCISE TWO:

1. Inference: The client feels she is not smart enough or educated enough to socialize with the people she meets at certain events.
   Clues: "nervous around a lot of people" "very educated types" "They are successful people" "And so smart."

2. Inference: The client is unhappy about the counselor's prospective absence.
   Clues: "I SUPPOSE" "even though you ARE the only one I can talk with."

3. Inference: The client believes that hanging around people his age will make him old, or, he is worried about aging and being around old people reminds him of his age.
   Clues: "don't want to hang around old people" "depressing" "intend to stay young"

4. Inference: The client is afraid the counselor will think he is crazy.
   Clues: "I'm not crazy" "I'm right in the head."

5. Inference: The client believes that placing her mother in a home is not loving her mother.
   Clues:, "People who love their mothers don't put them away." "only have one mother" "love and care for her."

READING 7
DIAGNOSIS OF BRAIN SYNDROME IN OLDER ADULTS

Probably, many of your older clients will be afraid they are losing their memories. It will be helpful for you to be familiar with assessment methods that can identify brain syndrome. This will make it possible for you to give accurate reassurance to many and to make appropriate medical referrals for others. Two assessment techniques will be explained: The Mental Status Questionnaire and The Face-Hand Test.

The Mental Status Questionnaire consists of ten reality questions. When you ask the client these questions, be sure the client and not their family answers. The following are the ten questions:

1. Where are you now? (What place is this? What is the name of this place? What kind of place is it?)

2. Where is it located? (approximate address)

3. What is the date today? The day of the week?

4. Month?

5. Year?

6. When were you born? Month?

7. Year of birth?

8. How old are you?

9. Who is the president of the United States?

10. Who was the president before him?

You may want to ask these additional questions:

1. Who am I?

2. What do I do? (What is my job called?)

3. Have you ever seen me before?

4. Where were you last night?

It is important to know, either from the client or their family, what medication the client was on and when he/she first began having memory problems.

The test is scored according to the number of errors on the first ten questions. A person's level of education can affect the results of these tests. Errors are more significant in a case where someone is highly educated, and less significant for someone who has had little education or who is not very intelligent.

55

Generally, the number of errors are interpreted as follows:

0-2 none or minimal brain syndrome
3-5 mild to moderate brain syndrome
6-8 at least moderate brain syndrome
9-10 severe organic brain syndrome

This test is only accurate when you're sure that the patient is not too deaf to hear you, when there is no real language difficulty, and when the patient is not antagonistic and resisting testing purposely. Also, someone who is highly anxious (you may notice them fidgeting, talking rapidly, asking questions over and over again, or pacing) may not even hear the questions you ask.

When you give the Face-Hand Test, instruct the client to sit facing you, hands face down on knees, and eyes closed. Then, with one finger gently but firmly touch one cheek and one hand simultaneously in the following pattern, asking the client to tell you where they are touched.

1. right cheek — left hand

2. left cheek — right hand

3. right cheek — right hand

4. left cheek — left hand

5. both cheeks

6. both hands

The first trial is a practice one. If the client only mentions a cheek or a hand, say "Where else?" Repeat this sequence a second time with the client's eyes closed and then a third time, with eyes open. After the practice trial, any errors are usually indicative of brain syndrome.

If these measures show any signs of brain syndrome, then refer the client to a medical doctor who can test for reversible problems, such as improper medication, infection, malnutrition, subdural hematoma.

There are certain other diagnostic facts which may be useful to you. They are listed here:

DIAGNOSTIC FACTS: (Butler)

1. Insight and depression may be present in the early phase of cerebral arteriosclerosis.

2. Depression may mask itself as organic confusion.

3. Reversible (acute) brain syndromes are often mis-diagnosed as chronic brain syndrome.

4. Acute and chronic brain syndromes may coexist.

5. Depression and brain syndromes may coexist.

6. Retinal arteriosclerosis is NOT diagnostic of cerebral arteriosclerosis.

7. Paradoxical excitatory drug reactions to barbituate sedatives may occur.

8. Tranquilizer-induced brain syndromes can occur.

9. Tranquilizer-induced depressions can occur.

HOMEWORK:

1. Give the MSQ and the Face-Hand Test to 10 people — at least 4 of them should be over age 70. Record your results:

Age	MSQ Errors	Face-Hand Errors after Practice Trial	Diagnostic Implications
1.			
2.			
3.			
4.			
5.			
6.			
7.			
8.			
9.			
10.			

2. If the people you test complain about their memory, ask them how long they have been having problems.

3. Ask each person what kind of medications they are currently taking.

READING 8
SEX AND THE OLDER ADULT

Sexual behavior can be influenced greatly by social and religious values and beliefs about sex and aging. Sex can be an enjoyable experience for most older adults. However, some older adults believe they are too old for sex, and our society ridicules others through sayings such as "the dirty old man" and jokes such as "Granny" in PLAYBOY. These false beliefs and negative attitudes make it difficult for some older adults to enjoy this natural, human way of relating.

When sex is not enjoyable and when this is considered a problem by the older person and/or the person's partner, this problem can be treated medically and psychologically. There are certain changes in sexual functioning which may be frightening to the older adult who does not understand them. When someone worries about their sexual functioning, it usually interferes with their enjoyment of sex and can also result in such functional problems as impotence. The following are changes which can occur with normal aging:

1. It takes longer for a man over 50 to get an erection than it did when the same man was 20 years old.

2. The older man usually needs more tactile stimulation to get an erection.

3. It takes an older man a longer time to have a climax than it does a younger man.

4. There is a higher incidence of impotence, usually psychogenic in origin, in older men. (Psychogenic means caused by psychological factors.)

5. It is normal for both older men and older women to have orgasms. With advancing age, it may become easier for a woman to experience orgasm.

6. After menopause, the lining of a woman's vagina may become drier and more delicate. This can make sexual intercourse painful. This problem can be treated by using additional lubrication and appropriate medication.

In general, if individuals have been active sexually as young and middle-aged adults, they can continue to be active in old age. Poor health can interfere, and poor health is more common in older adults. But poor health does not rule out sexual enjoyment. For example, after a person recovers from the crisis of a heart attack, sexual intercourse does not endanger his health.

The clinician should check for the following causes of impotence in older adults:

1) Certain drugs (especially for hypertension).
2) Boredom with sexual partner.
3) Not enough tactile stimulation.
4) Disease (e.g., diabetes).
5) Fear of old age and/or the belief that old age brings impotence.
6) Excessive use of alcohol.

The treatment of sexual inadequacy in adults is described clearly and scientifically in Masters and Johnson's HUMAN SEXUAL INADEQUACY.

QUIZ:

1. Is there sex after sixty?

2. Is it normal for women to have orgasms?

3. Name three instances where you have seen prejudice against sex in old age.

4. What age changes in sexual functioning might frighten an older man and lead to psychogenic impotence?

5. What might make intercourse painful for an older woman? Does she have to either live with this pain or give up sex?

6. If you are going to do sexual counseling, it is important that you understand your own values about sex. What are your feelings about the following?

a. Oral sex?

b. Talking about sex with your doctor?

c. Talking about sex with your sexual partner?

d. Anal sex?

e. Homosexuality?

f. Who should initiate sex?

g. Under what conditions do you consider sexual relations to be moral and proper?

For yourself?

For others?

h. Incest?

READING 9
PERSONALITY and AGING: BACKGROUND

Personality has been defined by Dr. Birren as the "characteristic way in which an individual responds to the events of adult life." There are two broad categories of such characteristic, individual responses. They are (1) inner and (2) outer.

(1) INNER responses are sometimes called covert or private. Inner responses are the ways we see ourselves, other people and events. They include our thoughts and feelings and our interpretations of what other people do and say. They also include our moods and our reasons (or motivations) which lead us to act in ways that are typical of us! We may or may not be aware of these things about ourselves, and we may or may not share them with others.

(2) OUTER responses are sometimes called overt or public. These responses involve other people in some way. For example, we may tend to move either toward or away from other people; to interact in a friendly or suspicious manner; to relate either actively or passively.

Perhaps this is the point to say something about the notion that personality is generally considered to be enduring in the sense that these patterns of inner and outer responses are thought to be relatively stable over time.

There are several theories about what determines personality. The basic determinants that have been studied are (1) heredity, (2) environment, (3) self. Heredity includes biology, physiology and any characteristics present at birth. Environment, when discussed as a determinant of personality, includes not only the physical environment, but also the individual's social, cultural and familiar environment. Some theories, such as the psychoanalytic ones, place more importance on the social environment of childhood than on the environment in which the adult lives. The category of determinants which are labelled "self" include an individual's self-concept and also the person's awareness of self-direction.

There are some assumptions which underlie many personality theories. One idea is that there are certain central themes in the organization of an individual's responses and that if you know what these are you will be able to predict future responses. According to this assumption, if you know what type of personality an individual has you will be able to understand him better, and you can, to some extent predict his behavior. This, of course, also presumes, as discussed earlier, that personality is relatively enduring over time, thereby making predictions possible.

Another way to look at personality is to see it as a process which intervenes between the events of adult life and one's behavior. A commonly used term is PERSONALITY TYPE. A personality type is a pattern or constellation of behavioral characteristics typically exhibited by some people. There are categories of these patterns which have been drawn to describe some of these types. Labeling people according to personality type, therefore, serves as a means for distinguishing individuals and leads to useful discussion and prediction.

Most developmental theories view personality as the result of both biology and social environment. Some theories are more biological than others. An example of a biological position would be that, at birth, some babies are more active or friendlier than others and that these differences are due to biological factors. An example of the social environment position would be that parental behavior (a part of one's social environment) can suppress or encourage the development of autonomous behavior in children.

One developmental theory which emphasizes self-concept presents the following hypothesis: Individuals develop a concept of who they are and then choose activities and interests which are congruent with that self-concept and hence perpetuate it. As individuals continue to do this across the life span, they become more of what they thought they were to begin with. This process is one explanation for the greater differentiation between individual personalities with advancing age.

In general, developmental theories support the view of stability of personality across the life span. If personality tends to remain the same, how can counseling effect a change? Those favoring environmental theories would say that personality can be affected by alterations in one's social and physical environment that result in learning, and, as a consequence, in behavioral changes. Hence, as a result of modifications in the relationships between a person and the situations which lead to positive or negative reinforcement, the characteristic clusters of that individual's behavior may change. Theorists who emphasize the role of self-awareness in personality development usually include the concept of self-determination in their theories. Therefore, counseling can effect changes in the person's self-concept by increasing the individual's self-awareness and making it possible for that individual to change if he or she chooses to do so. Although there seems to be measurable continuity of personality from early childhood onward, continual evolution of the personality over the life span would seem to characterize the healthy, adaptive adult.

QUIZ:

1. What are personality types?

2. In general, is personality stable across the life span?

3. What are the three basic determinants of personality that are usually studied?

4. Give a definition of personality.

5. Give examples of inner characteristic responses that can contribute to personality.

READING 10
PERSONALITY AND AGING: RESEARCH

The Berkeley Growth study looked at personality types in older adults. They found three personality types that were well-adjusted: (1) MATURE. They had a constructive approach to life and were neither excessively impulsive nor defensive. They moved easily into old age, accepting themselves and satisfied with activities and interpersonal relationships. (2) ROCKINGCHAIR. They leaned heavily on others, were passive and disengaged, and welcomed old age as a time to be free from responsibility and a time to indulge in dependency need-gratification. (3) ARMORED. They had well-developed defenses against the anxiety that can be aroused by the losses of aging. They warded off the dread of physical decline by keeping active. The Berkeley Growth Study found two types to be poorly adjusted: (1) ANGRY. They thought they had not achieved goals and felt disappointment and failure. They reacted with hostility and blamed others for their shortcomings and could not reconcile themselves to aging. (2) SELF-HATERS. They felt disappointment and failure over the past, too, but they blamed themselves and felt depressed, inadequate, and worthless. These personality types are not viewed as totally age related. One's style of adjustment in old age is related to one's previous personality.

The Kansas City Study described four personality types. They concluded that these personality styles were generally stable and that there are a variety of ways in which a relatively stable personality can successfully adjust and adapt to changes in role and status. The Kansas City Study did find evidence of changes in the covert aspects of personality. They found indications that people withdraw emotional investment with age, are less actively involved with the world, and can be preoccupied with their own inner life. They also noted a shift from active to passive mastery that occurs in late middle age. That is, older adults are more likely to see the world as controlling them. Additionally, they found interesting shifts in sex role perceptions: Women became more tolerant of aggressive impulses, and men became more tolerant of their own nurturant and affiliative impulses.

There have been a series of research studies done to determine whether DISENGAGEMENT or ACTIVITY lead to successful aging. The research has shown that neither one is right for everyone. Whether disengagement or activity adds to life-satisfaction for an older individual depends on that individual's particular personality and average level of activity across the life span.

Neugarten and her colleagues described four personality types that could be either active or disengaged in old age. (1) INTEGRATED. They are reorganizers who have a focus in their life whether they disengage or remain active. (2) UNINTEGRATED. They have difficulty restructuring and focusing their lives when they are faced with change and become apathetic and disorganized. (3) ARMORED-DEFENDED. They are focused reorganizers as long as they remain active. With inactivity, they tend to be constricted and seek others who will take care of them. (4) PASSIVE-DEPENDENT. They tend to live restricted lives and are dependent on others regardless of how active they are.

In closing, there is one significant factor that seems to aid successful adjustment across personality type. This is having a confidant. Having intimate, stable relationships where there is someone to really talk to serves as a buffer against the losses of aging.

QUIZ:

1. What personality type best describes you? Explain.

2. Which do you think you will prefer, activity or disengagement? Describe someone who has successfully adjusted using the style you do not prefer.

3. What factor can usually contribute to life satisfaction in old age?

4. How do sex roles change with aging?

Introducing the
Nine Step Counseling Model   6

    Every client enters into a counseling relationship with a goal in mind. Sometimes the goal is clearly defined and apparent to the client. Sometimes it is not. Whether or not the client can articulate his reason for seeing a counselor makes no difference. The very fact that he has entered the relationship implies a goal of some kind. Often a client comes to a counselor with a stated goal and after awhile finds that he really wants something else. This happens because counseling can open many unexplored areas for the client, and he may very well wish to explore them. In most instances counselees come to see a counselor because they want one or more of the following things: a) to solve a personal problem, b) to get help in making an important decision, c) because they are unhappy and don't know where else to go, d) to learn how to handle a difficult situation, e) to receive help, comfort and support during a crisis, f) to be able to converse with someone who is empathic and supportive, g) to learn more about themselves. Many times the client wants several of the above things from counseling. The Nine Step Counseling Model is a systematic approach designed to provide the counselor with skills and a framework with which he can meet the needs of most counselees. The Nine Steps in Counseling are:

1. Understanding the Client

2. Establishing Rapport

3. Defining the Problem

4. Setting a Goal

5. Clarifying Issues

6. Listing Alternatives

7. Exploring Alternatives

8. Supporting Decisions

9. Providing Closure

    Chapters One through Five concentrated on the first step, Understanding the Client. Chapter Six will attend to the second step, Establishing Rapport.

THE NINE STEP COUNSELING MODEL

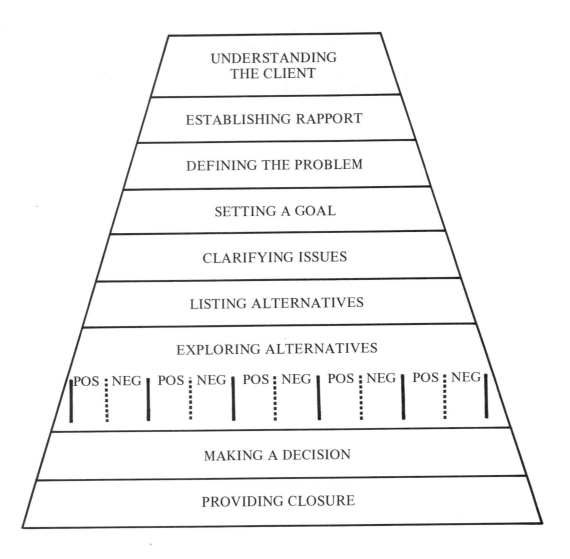

EXERCISE ONE: UNDERSTANDING RAPPORT

In order for a counselor to establish a facilitative relationship with a client, he must first establish a good rapport with that client. Establishing rapport requires that the counselor have empathy, respect and concern for the client. The terms "empathy," "respect," "concern" and "rapport" will be explained in this exercise.

DIRECTIONS FOR EXERCISE ONE:

Carefully read the definitions for the following terms. Give each term thoughtful consideration before passing on to the next one. After about fifteen minutes has passed the group should discuss the terms and their meanings with the leader.

EMPATHY: A counselor is empathic when he understands in the fullest way the counselee's deepest feeling, his frame of reference and his world-view. Empathy involves "feeling into and feeling with" the client. At moments when a person is truly and deeply empathic, he fuses with the thinking and feeling of the other person while maintaining the awareness that he is a separate person. To be empathically with someone is to be fully with him in his deepest moments.

RESPECT: When a counselor is respectful of the client, he truly believes in the worth of that client. He accepts the client AS HE IS. He may not like everything the client says or does, but he trusts that the client is the way he is for very good reasons. He respects the client for his humanness, and he conveys to the client his respect for the client's potential as a free individual.

CONCERN: When the counselor takes the client and his problem seriously, he is showing concern. The counselor also demonstrates concern when he is mentally and physically attentive to the client's communications. Concern for the client means being interested in his welfare and being willing to stick with the client even when the client is difficult to be with. Concern must be genuine. Since counselors are no less human than any other individual, it sometimes happens that the counselor cannot feel concern for a certain client, or cannot abide certain behavior. If this situation should arise, the counselor may want to work it through with the client, or refer the client to a different counselor.

RAPPORT: Rapport between counselor and client implies a relationship in which there is mutual trust and understanding. The client senses that the counselor has an empathic understanding of him and of his problem, and that the counselor accepts and respects who he is. He is also aware that the counselor is genuinely concerned about his welfare.

EXERCISE TWO: UNDERSTANDING EMPATHY

One way to develop better empathic skills is to improve your ability to become deeply involved in a fantasy. When a client is telling you something which is meaningful to him, it helps if you can picture what he is saying and listen in such a way that it seems as if you are having the experience.

DIRECTIONS FOR EXERCISE TWO:

Get yourself in a comfortable, relaxed position. Close your eyes and concentrate fully on what the group leader reads. The group leader will read a passage which describes a situation which is probably unfamiliar to you. The leader will read the passage very slowly, pausing for a while after each sentence. As you hear each sentence, picture in detail everything that happens in the sentence. Conjure a picture of what is happening. Notice the smells and the places involved and be very much in touch with the feelings and thoughts which accompany you as you experience what is happening in the passage. Remember that the story is about YOU. You are the individual in the passage.

PASSAGE:

You are sixty-seven years old. You work in a small grocery store where you have worked for twenty-two years. You are in charge of the produce department. You have developed a steady, efficient routine for ordering, inspecting and displaying the fruit and vegetables. You know most of the customers by name. Many of them you've known for years and they have become like friends to you. The owner of the store, a man you've known and liked for years, retires. His son takes over the store and hires a new manager, a recently graduated Business Major. After one week in the store he calls you to his office and tells you that he's restructuring the way the store is run. He intends to increase production and cut down waste. He has reviewed your schedule and has made certain changes. You are to work only in the back room, unpacking and processing the fruit and vegetables. You are to keep the back room clean. It will be more productive if another employee works in the front because he is less likely to get into conversations with the customers and will probably accomplish more. You are to check with him every time you order produce, even though you've been ordering the correct amount for twenty-two years. When you object he simply reminds you that things are different nowadays and it is important to improve productivity and use employees more efficiently. He hands you a xeroxed copy of your new assignments and tells you that you may go back to work. You leave his office.

QUESTIONS FOR CONSIDERATION:

1. Were you able to get into the fantasy?

2. If you were able to experience the fantasy, what feelings did you have during and after the reading of the passage?

3. Did the passage and the fantasy give you any new insights into a situation which is not unfamiliar to many older adults?

4. How would you respond to the following client statements?

   Client: "I've been working in 'Ready to Wear' for years. The manager changed the departments completely around. Now I have to work in 'Housewares.' I don't know anything about housewares and don't care to learn. I've got no say in anything that goes on around there."

   Response:

70

EXERCISE THREE: ESTABLISHING RAPPORT

The purpose of this exercise is to practice issuing responses which are intended to establish rapport with your client. Therefore, the types of desired responses are indicated after each client statement. Read the client statements and write the appropriate responses. The group may wish to discuss the members' responses and indicate why those responses help establish rapport.

1. Client: "I've been feeling very depressed lately. I've tried everything I know to get out of feeling this way. I'm not about to kill myself, but I sure wouldn't mind dying. When I was on the plane last month, I was actually hoping it would crash or something."

   Reflect Feelings:
   (empathy, respect)

   Reflect Content:
   (empathy)

   Statement of Concern:
   (empathy, respect)

2. Client: "I have never lived alone. I know if some burglar had come into the house when my husband was alive, he probably couldn't have done much. But nonetheless, now that he's passed on, I'm terrified to be alone at night. I haven't had a good night's sleep in months. I'm scared!"

   Reflect Feelings:
   (empathy, respect)

   Statement of Concern:
   (empathy, respect)

   Self-Disclose:
   (empathy-concern)

3. Client: "My problem is a sexual one. For awhile, about a year, I haven't been able to do anything. I just don't seem able to have an erection. I am very upset about this. I'm finding it hard to talk about it."

   Reflect Feelings:

   Statement of Concern:

   Statement to help make the client more comfortable:

4. Client: "I seem to change a lot. Sometimes I'm extremely high and happy and then I can be furious and not even know what I'm mad about. I go through a lot of moods and I don't understand why."

Reflect Content:

Reflect Feelings:

5. A middle aged woman brings her elderly mother in to speak with you. The daughter explains that her mother has become extremely forgetful and very cranky. The daughter is quite angry because the mother will not admit that she is forgetful or angry. The whole time the daughter is speaking to you the mother sits quietly, seeming to be disinterested in what the daughter is saying.

Respond to the Mother:
(Make your response one which is directed
at establishing rapport with the mother.)

EXERCISE FOUR: MAKING CONTACT and ESTABLISHING RAPPORT

The goal of this exercise is to establish a rapport with your partner. Choose a person whom you do not know well from the group. One member of the dyad is the speaker and the other member is the listener. The speaker attempts to relay "who he is" to the listener. This can be done by telling the listener how he feels about himself, how he feels about those around him, how he sees himself in relation to the important aspects of his life. When the speaker does this he is practicing self-disclosure. Therefore all of his communications should be Personal Communications. The listener attempts to repeat accurately what he believes the speaker said. The speaker lets the listener know if the listener has perceived him accurately. The listener should attempt to show concern and respect for the speaker. After ten minutes the roles are reversed and the exercise is begun again. When the entire exercise is completed the group and group leader discuss what was experienced and learned in the exercise.

HOMEWORK EXERCISES

EXERCISE ONE:

1. There are seven counselee goals listed at the beginning of Chapter Six. How many of them do you remember?

2. Establishing Rapport requires that the counselor have what three qualities?

3. When a counselor accepts a client AS HE IS, he is exhibiting what quality?

4. What are the nine steps of the Nine Step Counseling Model?

Check your answers with the answers provided on the last page of this chapter.

ANSWERS TO HOMEWORK QUESTIONS

Question I.
1. to solve a personal problem
2. to get help in making an important decision
3. because they are unhappy
4. to learn how to handle a difficult situation
5. to receive help, comfort and support during a crisis
6. to be able to converse with someone who is empathic and supportive
7. to learn more about themselves.

Question 2.
1. empathy
2. respect
3. concern

Question 3.
1. respect

Question 4.
1. Understand the Client
2. Establish Rapport
3. Define the Problem
4. Set a Goal
5. Clarify Issues
6. List Alternatives
7. Explore Alternatives
8. Support Decisions
9. Provide Closure

READING 11
PERSONALITY and AGING: DEVELOPMENTAL THEORIES

In this chapter several developmental theories and personality studies will be outlined. This is not meant to be an exhaustive review of this area. It is intended to provide you with some basic facts on this area of aging which you may integrate into your counseling.

BEUHLER'S THEORY OF THE COURSE OF HUMAN LIFE

Beuhler is psychoanalytically oriented and she studied the biographies and autobiographies collected in Vienna. She believes there is a biological basis for personality development which corresponds to a biological one of growth, culmination and decline. She focused on changes in MOTIVATION reflected in different goals at different stages of life. The following is her model:

STAGE	AGE	BIOLOGY	PHASE DESCRIPTION
Childhood	0-15	Progressive growth	Child at home prior to self-determination of goals
Youth	15-25	Continued growth with ability to reproduce sexually	Preparatory expansion (creative) experimental, tentative self-determination of goals. Choosing occupation and mate
Adult I	25-45	Stability of growth	Culmination: Continued creative expansion, maximal self-determination of goals. Time of occupational success and family development.
Adult II	45-65	Loss of reproductive ability	Self-assessment of the results of striving for goals: Upholding internal order, reassessing past goals and present situation, change in career or marriage partner is not unusual.
Aging	65+	Regressive growth and biological decline.	Experience of fulfillment or failure; continue previous activities but increasingly need to realize declining strengths, abilities; motivated by self-limitation; restricted goals to maintain stability; lack of self-determination and dependency.

ERICKSON'S EIGHT STAGES OF MAN

Erickson's life span theory builds on Freud's psychoanalytic theory of development. It is a psychosocial theory; Erickson views development as a progressive resolution of conflicts between an individual's needs and social demands. He identified eight developmental stages, each of which has a key psychological task or conflict. Failure to resolve a conflict makes it practically impossible to move to the next stage.

The following is Erickson's model:

AGE	STAGE	THEORETICAL CONFLICT
0-2	oral/sensory	TRUST vs MISTRUST: This involves practical problems for the infant such as feeding and weaning. Will the infant's needs be satisfied by adults or not? The development of HOPE is important at this stage.
2-3	anal	AUTONOMY vs SHAME: The practical problem at this stage is toilet training. The child has feelings of self-control warring with shame over lack of control and competence. In this stage WILL-POWER can develop.
4-5	phallic	INITIATIVE vs GUILT: The practical problem here is the Oedipal (or Electra) complex: physical attraction to the parent of the opposite sex. This is resolved by identification with parent of same sex. Lack of resolution leads to harsh responses by the parents to the child's sexual initiations which develops guilt. At this stage, sex-role identification and a sense of purpose can be developed.
6	latency	INDUSTRY vs INFERIORITY: At this stage, the individual learns to work together with others to develop intellectual skills, to demonstrate mastery in school and, hence, develop a sense of competence. Resolution at this stage is hindered by lack of praise for successes and results in feelings of inferiority.
Female 11-19 Male 13-19	genital	IDENTITY vs ROLE DIFFUSION: The practical problem here is learning an adult role, defining oneself as an adult, discovering one's attitudes and values leading to a sense of morality, and developing a sense of self-consistency.
20-30	young adulthood	INTIMACY vs ISOLATION: The conflict is between commitment to another vs self-absorption, fear of others and seeing others as a threat. This is the stage in which the individual usually chooses a mate and an occupation. It is time for the development of LOVE.

AGE	STAGE	THEORETICAL CONFLICT
30-55	adulthood	GENERATIVITY vs STAGNATION: The practical problems are establishing and guiding the next generation, making children productive, developing altruistic concerns. The conflict is occupational achievement and creativity vs boredom and self-preoccupation.
55+	later maturity	INTEGRITY vs DESPAIR: The problem is one of accepting one's own and only life. Evaluating one's life and seeing that it has been meaningful vs a sense of meaninglessness. There is a sense that time is short; it's the time of retirement and decline of health. This stage can develop WISDOM.

HAVIGHURST'S DEVELOPMENTAL TASKS AND DOMINANT CONCERNS*

Havighurst's model is based on social expectations and culture. He postulates that the phases occur earlier for the working class than for the middle class but with the same sequence. In his life span model, each decade of life is characterized by a dominant concern which orients behavior during that period.

The following is Havighurst's model:

AGE	CONCERN	DEVELOPMENTAL TASKS
0-10	Coming into independent existence	
10-20	Becoming a person in one's own mind. (Being acceptable)	(1) achieve relations with others (2) achieve masculine/feminine social roles (3) achieve independence from parents (4) choose/prepare for vocation (5) achieve socially responsible behavior (6) establish ethics, values (7) develop physical/mental abilities
20-30	Focusing one's life. (Maximum concern with oneself and personal life)	(1) choosing a mate (2) getting started and establishing a career, occupation (3) starting a family (4) managing a home
30-40	Collecting one's energies (Stable time)	(1) Civic and social responsibility (2) establish and maintain adequate standard of living (3) assist children to become responsible (4) leisure activities (5) marriage relationship develops

AGE	CONCERN	DEVELOPMENTAL TASKS
50-60	Creating a new lifestyle (Doubts about occupational. IQ, Social, physical powers)	(6) accept physical changes (7) deal with aging parents (8) Experimentation with new careers, marriage relationship, activities
60-70	Deciding whether to disengage and how	(1) adjust to declining physical health (2) adjust to retirement and lower income (3) death of spouse (4) establish satisfying living arrangement (5) wisdom, acceptance of life

*FOOTNOTE:

Kimmel, P. C. *Adulthood and Aging: An interdisciplinary developmental view.* New York: John Wiley and Sons, 1974.

MASLOW: HIERARCHY OF NEEDS AND SELF-ACTUALIZATION

Maslow focuses on healthy personality development which he sees as proceeding from physiological and instinctive determinants of behavior to more rational and cognitive determinants. He presents a hierarchy of human needs. Gratification of a particular need leads to a temporary state of happiness, followed by a new need that must be satisfied. He proposes the concept of self-actualization; people tend toward becoming all they can be; the goal of life is to realize all your potential once basic needs are met.

The following is Maslow's developmental model:

AGE	NEED	DEFINITION OF NEED
Infant	Physiological	Physical needs for water, food, shelter
Young Child	Safety	Protection from threat and danger
Adolescent	Belongingness and Love	Intimate relations with same and opposite sex, others
Adult	Esteem	Respect, admiration of others because of competence and achievements.
Middle Age +	Self-actualization	Need to become all that one can be; need to know and understand (wisdom)

QUIZ:

1. Which developmental theory do you prefer? How does your own life fit into this model so far?

2. Beuhler's theory of personality development is one of (a)_____,
   (b) _____ , and (c)_____and it parallels
   (d) _____ development.

3. The ultimate stage of development is Maslow's theory is _____ .

4. According to Erickson, what are the conflicts to be resolved in adulthood and old age?

READING 12
CLINICAL INFORMATION

Although you, as a counselor, are not expected to have the same knowledge and understanding of clinical information as a psychologist or psychiatrist, it will be helpful to be familiar with some basic clinical facts. Briefly, this reading will cover stress, life review, depression, and suicide.

One area where there can be a change with age is in response to stressful situations. This is because biologically lower resistance to stress is a part of normal aging (Kral).

It is not uncommon for older persons to engage in a process called LIFE REVIEW. Life review involves a tendency to reminisce, to tell stories, and to think of past events. This process serves a useful function. It helps the individual to integrate his/her life in a meaningful way. You and your client may want to integrate this process into part of your counseling.

There is an increased incidence of depression in old age. The following are signs which can alert you to the possibility of depression:

1. feelings of guilt

2. feelings of worthlessness

3. loneliness

4. boredom

5. constipation

6. sexual disinterest

7. impotence

8. fatigue

9. insomnia

10. physical complaints

Along with this higher incidence of depression, there are more suicides in old age, especially in white males over the age of 65. It is important to take suicide threats seriously when they occur. The myth that people who threaten suicide never kill themselves is just that, A MYTH. However, older individuals do not always make a plea for help through a suicide threat. The following are other indications that a person is considering suicide:

1. depression

2. withdrawal

3. bereavement

4. isolation — widowed, single

5. expectation of death from some cause

6. less organization and complexity of behavior

7. induced helplessness

8. institutionalization

9. physical illness

10. decreased self-regard

11. desire and rational decision to protect survivors from financial disaster

12. philosophical decision — no more pleasure or purpose in life.

13. organic mental deterioration

14. changes in sleep pattern — nightmares

15. males over 65

QUIZ:

1. What are two clinical problems that increase in frequency with advancing age?

2. What is LIFE REVIEW?

3. If a client feels bored, tired and worthless, what might this indicate?

4. Reread the suicide indicators.

5. Some people believe that each individual has the right to decide if he/she wants to die. Others think it is never right to commit suicide. What are your beliefs?

Setting Counseling Goals 7

The counseling session has several features which distinguish it from other modes of human interaction. One obvious feature concerns communication styles. The communication which takes place in the Counseling Session is, for the most part, personal communication. The fact that the counseling session has certain goals and objectives also adds to its uniqueness. The counselor and client establish a very special kind of relationship and work together to accomplish a mutually agreed upon goal. The following exercises are intended to clarify the concept of goal formation. Developing the skill of accurate goal setting will be of great help to counselors who want their counseling to be focused and purposeful.

There is one last note on goal formation which is important to remember. Deciding on a goal for counseling is primarily the prerogative of the client. If the client's goal is not agreeable to you then you will need to negotiate with the client and attempt to come to some mutual agreement. If no agreement can be reached, you should consider the wisdom of setting up a counseling relationship where such a problem exists. Setting a goal in counseling is so fundamental that lack of agreement on this issue can only harm the relationship and detract from the effectiveness of your counseling.

EXERCISE ONE: DEFINING THE PROBLEM

Defining a client's problem is very similar to reflecting content. It requires listening for the central issue to emerge from the client's communications to you. Many times, however, the client has multiple problems. Often his problem is so complex that many issues and problem areas arise during the course of discussion. When this occurs, divide the problem into manageable components and ask the client which of those components he would like to discuss first. When one problematic situation has been discussed and defined, the counselor and client move onto the next step, that of clarifying the issues involved in the problem.

DIRECTIONS FOR EXERCISE ONE:

Read the following client statements. Summarize the content and state possible client feelings. Formulate a response which is a statement of the client's problem. Do NOT fill in the spaces marked Set Goal or Clarify Issues. After you have completed the exercise, compare and discuss your answers with the group and the group leader. Suggested answers to this exercise can be found at the end of the chapter. Before beginning the exercise, read and study EXAMPLE A.

EXAMPLE A:

Client: "I received a telegram this morning from my mother. She said my Dad is dying. The doctors believe he will live only a few days longer. My Dad and I have never gotten along. We haven't spoken in years. I guess both of us are pretty stubborn. Now that he's dying, I'm feeling awful. I think I care about him more than I ever realized. I don't want him to die with things the way they are between us."

Content: Woman's father is dying. She and her father are not on good terms. She does not like the situation.

Feelings: sadness, anxiety, frustration, confusion, fear, regret, guilt.

Definition of Problem: "You are very unhappy that your father is dying and you haven't made up with him."

Goal: For the counselee to find a way in which she can do something that will make her feel better about her relationship with her dying father.

Issues: Her feelings about her father — her feelings about talking to him — his possible reaction to her — her feelings about his dying — her stubbornness — his stubbornness.

1. Client: "There are really so many problems and things to consider. If we move my mother-in-law, where do we move her to? If we leave her with us, then what about the situation with the kids? And then there's my husband. Harry would think we're abandoning her. I just don't know what to do about it."

Write Content:

List Feelings:

Define Problem:

Set Goal:

Clarify Issues:

84

2. Client: "Taking care of her can be unbearable at times. Sometimes I feel like walking out and leaving it all behind. Never returning. But, you know, I really wouldn't do that. I still love her, and she was such a good wife to me all those years."

Write Content:

List Feelings:

Define Problem:

Set Goal:

Clarify Issues:

3. Client: "I don't seem to want to go anywhere anymore. You see, I don't hear so well and it's embarrassing to keep asking people what they said to me. I'm not sure anymore about what's going on around me. But, when I stay home and don't go out, I get very depressed."

Write Content:

List Feelings:

Define Problem:

Set Goal:

Clarify Issues:

4. Client: "He doesn't understand. There's not enough for me to do around the house anymore. Anyway, why keep the place spotless if there's no one to notice? It would be different if my husband appreciated the things that I do. But he doesn't. He never really did. When I complain that I'm bored, he just gives me a lecture about how lucky I am that I don't have to go to work every day. Maybe he's right. But if I'm so lucky, how come I feel so rotten?"

Write Content:

List Feelings:

Define Problem:

Set Goal:

Clarify Issues:

5. Client: "Last year my husband took sick rather suddenly. He died three days later. It was a terrible shock to me and for awhile I thought I'd never get through it. I

feel a lot stronger now, but I still have problems with it. I have a feeling deep down that something will happen and I won't be able to handle it. I miss him a lot. I can't get used to not having him around."

Write Content:

List Feelings:

Define Problem:

Set Goal:

Clarify Issues:

EXERCISE TWO: SETTING GOALS

Once the client's problem has been defined, setting a goal is a simple matter. Simply turn the problem around, and make its solution the goal of the counseling session. For example, in Exercise One, EXAMPLE A, the woman's problem was one of dissatisfaction with her relationship to her dying father. The counselling GOAL was that of finding a way for her to feel better about that relationship. In a subsequent chapter we shall see how the goal is accomplished. For the present, however, all that you are required to do is return to Exercise One and formulate a GOAL for each client.

EXERCISE THREE: CLARIFYING ISSUES

If people's problems were always simple and clear, they would rarely need the help of others in order to solve them. What we refer to in this chapter as "issues" are those things which accompany problems and make solutions more difficult and complicated. When the woman in Example A received a telegram that her father was dying, there was a problem. Why? The answer, of course, is because she was on very bad terms with him at the time. This complicated the normal procedure whereby she could simply go visit him before he died. Would her visit upset him? Would her not going upset him? What would she say to him? How would he react to her? Would the visit be unbearably anxiety provoking for her? How would she feel after he died if she did not visit him? All of these questions are the issues which accompany her problem. Notice how many issues revolve around her FEELINGS! When considering issues in any client's problem, always consider the feelings the person has about the problem.

DIRECTIONS FOR EXERCISE THREE:

Return to Exercise One. List the issues involved in the problems of the five clients. When the entire group has finished all three exercises, discuss and compare answers. There are suggested answers at the end of the chapter. There can be several answers to each question so do not consider your answer incorrect if it differs somewhat from the answers given by the authors.

EXERCISE FOUR: PRACTICING GOAL SETTING

One or more group members volunteer to share a problematic situation in their lives. The group members who volunteer are taking the role of the client. The remainder of the group acts as the counselor. As each volunteer shares his problem, the group listens very carefully. When the client-volunteer has finished explaining his story, the group answers the following questions:

1. How would you define the client's problem?

2. What issues are involved in his problem?

3. What "counseling goals" would you suggest?

HOMEWORK EXERCISES

EXERCISE ONE:

Is there anything happening in your life at the present which is a problem for you? If so, write a description of it which resembles Client Statements in the exercises. It will make it simpler if you can imagine that you are telling it to someone. After you have written your problem, extract the content, list the feelings, define the problem, set a counseling goal for yourself, and list the issues involved in the goal. Study what you have written. Does writing it out in this manner help you see some aspects of the problem which you have failed to see in the past?

EXERCISE TWO:

If some one in your family, a friend or an acquaintance should tell you about a problem they are having, do with their problem what you did with your own. See if you can gain some insights which you can share with them concerning their problem.

SUGGESTED ANSWERS TO EXERCISES

EXERCISE ONE:

1. Content: Client does not know where her mother-in-law should live.
   Feelings: confused, anxious, apprehensive, conflicted, discouraged, frustrated, guilty, helpless, pressured, uneasy, unhappy.
   Statement of Problem: "The problem as I see it is that you can not decide where your mother-in-law should live."

2. Content: Client is experiencing difficulty in caring for his wife. He is also ambivalent about caring for her.
   Feelings: angry, resentful, guilty, confused, ambivalent, hurting, fed-up, helpless, uneasy, unappreciated.
   Statement of Problem: "It seems to me that even though you love your wife, you are having difficulty caring for her."

3. Content: Client is embarrassed because she cannot hear, so she tends to stay at home. Staying at home alone depresses her.
   Feelings: lonely, depressed, sad, helpless, hopeless, frustrated, embarrassed, insecure, unhappy.
   Statement of Problem: "You stay at home because your hearing is so bad. Staying home depresses you."

4. Content: Client is bored and feeling useless. She believes her husband does not appreciate her.
   Feelings: hurt, angry, resentful, despondent, unappreciated, unloved, discouraged, useless, helpless, unhappy.
   Statement of Problem: "You are dissatisfied with your life the way it is. Also you are not feeling understood and appreciated by your husband."

5. Content: The client is having a difficult time adjusting to her husband's death.
   Feelings: lonely, sad, unhappy, fearful, helpless, hopeless, hurt, insecure, afraid.
   Statement of Problem: "You are feeling lost without your husband and having a difficult time adjusting to his being gone."

EXERCISE TWO:

1. The counseling goal is to help the client decide where her mother-in-law should live.

2. The counseling goal is to help the client find a way to make caring for his wife less difficult for him.

3. The counseling goal is to help the client have contact with others even though she has difficulty hearing.

4. The counseling goal is two-fold. One goal is to help her find ways to make her life more fulfilling. The other goal is to improve communications between her and her husband.

5. The counseling goal is to find ways of helping the client adjust to her husband's death. Another goal would be helping her to find a meaningful life without her husband.

EXERCISE THREE:

1. Issues: problems which arise with mother-in-law and the children, problems arising from finding a proper home, husband's feelings about having his mother leave, possible feelings of guilt on the part of the client, feelings of mother-in-law about leaving, financial capabilities of family.

2. Issues: length and severity of his wife's illness, severity of his frustration, his anger, his resentment, his love for her, his sense of loyalty and appreciation for her.

3. Issues: extent of client's hearing loss, extent of her embarrassment, the attitudes of her friends toward her hearing losses, the severity of her depression, the extent of her support group.

4. Issues: the extent of client's feelings of uselessness, the possibility of client developing new interests, the willingness of client's husband to improve communication patterns, the severity of her depression, the severity of the marriage problem.

5. Issues: severity of her depression, the extent of her support system, the extent of her loneliness and fearfulness, the extent of her progression through the stages of mourning.

READING 13
SPECIAL ISSUES IN LATE ADULTHOOD

Each period of life presents us with developmental tasks to be accomplished. These tasks and the time in which they are to be completed can be seen most clearly in infancy and childhood. Dr. Spock has outlined some of the biologically-based ones, such as when most children learn to walk. One norm which is set by society is that children begin their formal educational task between the ages of 4 and 6. The time frame for most developmental tasks tends to broaden with advancing age. For example, most individuals chose their faith, their occupation, and their spouse during the first third of their life. Of course, there are exceptions.

One of the socially-determined developmental tasks of old age in America is retirement. The time for this task is influenced by the age of forced retirement in some jobs and the age at which social security benefits can be collected. Retirement can be a relief or a crisis. One problem, often not anticipated, can be the changes it brings to family living. In the traditional couple, where the husband earned the living while the wife kept the house, the retiring husband may find himself "underfoot" when he is home all day, every day. As a result, he may not only be depressed because he no longer has his status as the breadwinner of the family, but he may also feel that he does not belong anywhere. Since retirement is one of the tasks of late-adulthood, adults can avoid some of its potential problems by planning ahead for their retirement years. As a counselor you can help by leading pre-retirement discussion groups where soon-to-retire employees can talk to each other about the changes that come with retirement.

Women who raise families experience a change similar to retirement. This occurs when their children grow up and leave home. This time is called the empty nest.

An older individual is more likely to be separated from his/her friends and relatives. As the years go by his/her friends and relatives move away or die. Many women outlive their husbands and find themselves alone and grieving. Widowhood is more difficult for the person who does not understand the grief process. It is a normal part of grieving to be stunned and disbelieving and to be angry at the person who has died — as well as to feel sorry and eventually feel the loss less and less. Some people feel conflict and guilt about their angry feelings which are a natural part of grieving. As a counselor, you can be of help by sharing information about the stages of grief: disbelief, anger, sorrow, and resolution.

These stages of grief are similar to the process a person goes through when faced with his/her own death. As a person ages, the inevitability of death comes closer. That person may want to talk over his fears with someone, but they may find that their fears make others so anxious that they try to talk them away rather than listen. It can be easier to say, "No, don't worry about dying. You're not going to die," than it is to listen to someone's fears about death because they make you face your own.

QUIZ:

1. Are the developmental issues of old age similar to those of childhood?

2. What types of issues arise more frequently in late middle age and old age?

3. What are the stages of grief?

4. What do you plan to do when you retire, or your children grow up? Or, how has your life changed since you have retired and/or since your children have grown up?

READING 14
COUNSELING THE DYING AND THE GRIEVING   Janet Witkin, M.A.

   We all know we are going to die one day, yet this "knowing" is far from most of our thoughts most of the time. In recent years, people have been helping dying people work through their feelings about their lives and their deaths, as well as helping the survivors of intimate deaths — wives, husbands, children, parents, friends — deal with their feelings about the passing of their loved ones.

   Dr. Elisabeth Kübler-Ross, a pioneer in working with dying people, tells us that one of the most important gifts we can give a dying patient or her/his family member or friend is our deepest, authentic presence. In order to do this, we must first deal with our own mortality, our own feelings about death. One way to attempt to do this is to fantasize your own death and funeral, to really visualize what it will be like. Another way is to write your own obituary and your own epitaph. With both these exercises, it's important to really let yourself feel whatever comes up within you; there is no right or wrong way to feel. You may think of other creative ways to put yourself in touch with your own death. This may be difficult for you, but it will help you understand what others may go through when they learn that their death is imminent.

   Dr. Kübler-Ross also tells us that dying people can easily spot phoniness in the people around them. So, deep authenticity is required of those working effectively with the dying.

   In her book ON DEATH AND DYING, Dr. Kübler-Ross describes five stages that most dying people go through when they learn that they're dying: 1) denial and isolation, 2) anger, 3) bargaining, 4) depression, 5) acceptance. Of course, not all people will go through all stages, and not necessarily in the same order. But, it is helpful to be familiar with these stages so that, for example, one can understand that a dying person's anger towards you, at a given moment, may be about her/his dying and your living, your not dying — and that it's no more personal than that.

   In counseling dying people, it is so important that we accept the individual's way of dealing with her/his dying — be it within a Christian, Jewish, Moslem, Buddhist, Hindu, atheist, or agnostic framework. IT DOES NOT MATTER. A person must be given the space to die as they have lived. If a human being has lived as a dreamer, she/he has the right to die as a dreamer (denier, romantic, etc.). It's so important to accept a person where she/he is, not pushing or persuading or enticing them to believe as we do, but providing opportunities, spaces, silences for them to venture into a discussion of their feelings — or just to be — perhaps silently — in our presence.

   Our basic challenge — be it with a dying person or the survivor of an intimate death — is TO BE PRESENT — deeply, authentically, acceptingly, humanly, warmly present.

   Just as there are stages a dying person goes through, there are also stages that the survivor of an intimate death goes through. Robert E. Kavanaugh in FACING DEATH, describes seven phases in the grieving process, stages that one who has lost a loved one will probably experience, but not necessarily all of them and not necessarily in this order. The seven stages are: 1) shock, 2) disorganization, 3) volatile emotions, 4) guilt, 5) loss and loneliness, 6) relief, and 7) re-establishment. Each stage is accompanied by somewhat predictable emotions and behaviors. The counselor who is sensitive to the stages of grief can be helpful by understanding the griever's needs at each stage.

   1) SHOCK: A person's first reaction to the death of a loved one is physical and emotional shock; real and unreal worlds collide. Strange behavior and conversation are common. Shortly after the initial shock, disbelief or various other forms of denial may

begin. During the period of shock and denial, the best role for the counselor is one of physical presence and touch, and permissive listening. Also, a few words of reassurance may need to be repeated, as they may not be heard the first time. Though you'll probably be tempted to give advice, explanations, or religious clichés, these are not helpful at this time. The counselor's role is to keep the griever in touch with a supportive, caring part of the world.

2) DISORGANIZATION: The second stage in human grief is one of disorganization, one in which the grieving person may claim to feel totally out of touch with the ordinary proceedings of life. The basic need of the griever at this stage is for the consistent physical presence of someone they can trust. They need gentle, caring physical contact — hugging, handholding, caressing, rubbing — to assure them of the existence of a gentle and pleasureful world. They may need to cry and cry, to talk and talk, with seemingly little connection to reality. It's not our role to interrupt them with our reasoning, but to let their crying and/or talking run its natural course; what they are doing can be quite helpful and clarifying for them. Important decisions about the future should be postponed until disorganization fades.

3) VOLATILE EMOTIONS: The third stage in the dynamics of human grief, when mourners may unleash their volatile emotions, can be quite upsetting to those around them. Behind the rage, resentment, hatred, jealousy, or terror that may be directed toward the newly dead, may be the griever's more primary feelings of helplessness, pain, and frustration. A counselor needs to touch these primary feelings, as well as permissively listening to and accepting any and all other feelings. Doctors, nurses, clergy, God, relatives (and counselors?) may be whipping posts used by the mourner. The counselor needs to accept all feelings and assure the mourner that such violent and strange feelings are okay and will pass.

4) GUILT: The fourth stage mourners experience is one of guilt. The counselor's role here is one of patient, permissive, non-judgmental listening, which gives the griever the space to work through their guilt. The counselor's listening and acceptance may allow the grieving person to forgive her/himself.

5) LOSS AND LONELINESS: The sense of loss and loneliness in the fifth stage of grief may well be the most painful. The little things that were so familiar are gone or painfully different — the empty chair or side of the bed, the extra toothbrush, photographs, missing phone calls, conversations, kisses. As the sense of loss grows, self-pity, sadness, and depression may follow. Loneliness seems unbearable at this time; the heart's vacuum cannot be filled. The frequent and regular presence of a stabilizing friend is so necessary at this point. The griever needs courage and endurance to allow her/himself to fully experience the depth and meaning of the lost relationship. Keeping busy or jumping into new relationships may appear to be cures, but completing grieving is really the task at hand.

6) RELIEF: The sixth stage, one characterized by feelings of relief, may be difficult for the mourner to admit and acknowledge openly. Relief is natural after being with a loved one throughout a long illness. It is also natural to feel relief because death frees us from demands and pressures and opens up for us new possibilities and opportunities. Relief is normal and must be acknowledged as such. The counselor must be able to listen acceptingly to the griever's sense of relief without indicting or adding to guilt or shame. The mourner most needs to express freely her/his feelings of relief. Such relief is normal and does not imply a lack of love for the dead person.

7) RE-ESTABLISHMENT: The final stage, which does not come all at once, is re-establishment. Friends are so important at this stage — both new and old friends. Grievers should be allowed to set their own pace during this time, and not be pushed by others. The mourner knows best when to do what.

Of course, each person will go through grieving at her/his own pace and in her/his unique style. After lengthy dying, grieving may not take as long as it does after a sudden or unexpected death. However, the intimate other of a person who has a long illness needs support during the months and years of the illness. After sudden or unexpected death, comforting may be needed long after callers have stopped coming.

With the elderly, the grieving process may begin long before the death occurs — anticipatory grief. We may begin to grieve for someone when we notice they're growing old or ill.

Robert Kavanaugh also mentions the value of bringing humor to the mourner, the kind of natural humor that gives one that marvelous sense of perspective, that allows one to take an aerial or cosmic view of one's own situation — and to smile at one's own foibles and those of loved ones.

QUIZ:

1. What may a person need during the disorganization stage of grief?

2. What psychological stages do most dying people go through?

3. What is the most important thing you have to give a dying person?

4. What is anticipatory grief?

Exploring Alternatives 8

All of us at times find ourselves in a position of having to make an important personal decision. Being aware of the obvious alternatives does not always make the decision easier. Sometimes in fact, the more alternatives there are, the more difficult it is to make a decision. Usually we have friends and relatives who are more than eager to give us strong, incisive advice. How often have you heard someone say to a friend or relative, "Leave him, he's no good for you anyway!" These kinds of advice givers are always abundant, but very rarely are they taken seriously. The reason for this is that that type of advice is far more simplistic than the problem. Life isn't simple and most important personal decisions are complex. Sometimes people get depressed and lose hope because their situations seem so complex that they fear there is no way out. Such complex problems can be broken down into manageable components. Chapters Seven, Eight and Nine of this manual present a model which makes problem solving easier for the client and the counselor. Chapter Seven presented a method of narrowing and defining the problem. This chapter will concentrate on studying the complexities of a problematic situation and then formulating possible alternative solutions.

EXERCISE ONE: LISTING ALTERNATIVES

An alternative is a choice. In the last chapter the counselor and client examined the client's problem and formulated a counseling goal. The goal was the natural outgrowth of the problem. For example, the woman who was having difficulty because she was on bad terms with her dying father, decided, with the aid of the counselor, that her goal would be "finding something she could do which would make her feel better about her relationship with her dying father."

ALTERNATIVES are STEPS the client could take to achieve his GOAL. The following section of this exercise outlines a method which you can use to help your client formulate alternatives.

DIRECTIONS FOR EXERCISE ONE:

Read the following section slowly and thoughtfully. When you have finished reading, discuss what you have read with the group and group leader.

A METHOD FOR LISTING ALTERNATIVES

One: State the counseling goal. Read it carefully with your client so that you can be sure that you both understand what the goal implies and mutually agree that it is an appropriate goal for the present.

Two: Ask the client to list all the possible ways (alternatives) he can think of to achieve that goal. (NOTE: the client will be hesitant to list alternatives he does not like. Remind him that this is just an exercise and listing alternatives does NOT mean that he will have to act on them.)

Three: After the client has exhausted his list of possible alternatives, add alternatives which the client omitted. (NOTE: It is very helpful to make a written list of alternatives.)

EXERCISE TWO: EXPLORING ALTERNATIVES

DIRECTIONS FOR EXERCISE TWO:

Read the following section slowly and thoughtfully. When you have finished reading, discuss what you have read with the group and group leader.

Once the counselor and client have listed alternatives, the next stage of the counseling model is the exploration of these alternatives. This exploration involves examining the positive and negative consequences of any alternative the client may wish to choose. A POSITIVE CONSEQUENCE is a RESULT which makes the client feel good, is compatible with the client's world-view, and has beneficial practical results. A NEGATIVE CONSEQUENCE is one which makes the client feel bad, clashes with his world-view, and has detrimental practical results. (An alternative is the same as a choice. Often we will be referring to an alternative as a choice.)

The following example is an illustration of positive and negative aspects of a choice. Suppose a client wants to change her life in some significant way because she is not satisfied with it the way it is. If one of her alternatives is to return to school to work toward a degree, the counselor would help her examine this particular alternative.

ALTERNATIVE: Returning to School

POSITIVE CONSEQUENCES

Sense of accomplishment
    (feeling)

Ability to earn more money
in the future
    (practical results)

Better self-esteem
    (a belief that a degree increases self-worth is a part of the client's world-view.)

NEGATIVE CONSEQUENCES

Anxiety and tension
    (feelings about returning to school)

Expense and time consumption
    (practical results)

Spending less time with children.
    (guilt, resulting from belief that mothers should spend much time with children, a part of client's world-view.)

Because nearly all choices have positive and negative consequences, it is important to examine the consequences with the client before the client attempts to make a decision concerning a course of action to choose.

The discussion of positive and negative consequences is an important and often lengthy part of the counseling process. It is during this phase that the counselor enlists all of the skills he has acquired in the preceding chapters. While being empathic and supportive of the client, the counselor uses his responding skills to explore the client's feelings and world-view at much deeper levels. Because a client's feelings and world-view are so potent, the counselor will find that the client will often forego obvious positive practical consequences rather than violate their feelings or belief system. Thus, it often happens that an older adult will go to incredible extremes to care for an ailing spouse rather than entrust the partner to the care of another person or institution. Why do people so often do this? Most of the time it is because they would rather suffer severe inconveniences than suffer guilt. Their world-view contains a belief that not caring for a partner is tantamount to deserting that partner and loving him less. Therefore, you can understand why we emphasize the examination of feelings and beliefs during this stage of counseling. We would like at this point to also emphasize the importance of respecting world-views and feelings of the client, no matter how much they vary from your own.

A METHOD FOR EXAMINING ALTERNATIVES

One: State the alternative.

ALTERNATIVE

Return to School

Two: List Positive and Negative consequences.

Positive	Negative
accomplishment	anxiety, tension
money	work and expense
self-esteem	seeing children less

Three: Discuss in depth with your client, all the items listed under positive and negative consequences.

*Items listed under ISSUES in the last chapter on page 90 will be very helpful for deciding consequences.

EXERCISE THREE: PRACTICING THE EXPLORATION OF ALTERNATIVES

The group leader refers to Chapter Seven, Exercise One. He reads aloud the statement of Client One. The group listens carefully as the leader reads the client's statement. When the reading is finished, the group comments on possible client feelings, issues involved in the statement, and sets a counseling goal. The group members write the goal, list possible alternatives, and write positive and negative consequences where indicated on this and following pages. When the group has done so for Client One, the leader then proceeds to read aloud Client Two's statement from the same exercise. The group and Leader continue the same proceedure for all five clients. It is helpful if the group does Clients One and Two AS a group, and then fills in required information for Clients Three to Five on their own. At the end of the exercise the group and leader should discuss the answers of various group members.

1. Client One: Counseling Goal _____

_____

Alternatives:

1. _____

2. _____

3. _____

4. _____

Client One:

Alternative One			Alternative Two		
Positive		Negative	Positive		Negative

Alternative Three			Alternative Four		
Positive		Negative	Positive		Negative

2. Client Two: Counseling Goal _____

_____

Alternatives:

1. _____

2. _____

3. _____

4. _____

Client Two:

Alternative One			Alternative Two		
Positive		Negative	Positive		Negative

Alternative Three			Alternative Four		
Positive		Negative	Positive		Negative

Client Three: Counseling Goal _____

_____

Alternatives:

1. _____

2. _____

3. _____

4. _____

Client Three:

Alternative One		
Positive		Negative

Alternative Two		
Positive		Negative

Alternative Three		
Positive		Negative

Alternative Four		
Positive		Negative

Client Four: Counseling Goal _____

                   _____

                   Alternatives:

                   1. _____

                   2. _____

                   3. _____

                   4. _____

Client Four:

Alternative One

Positive	Negative

Alternative Two

Positive	Negative

Alternative Three

Positive	Negative

Alternative Four

Positive	Negative

Client Five: Counseling Goal _____

_____

Alternatives:

1. _____

2. _____

3. _____

4. _____

Client Five:

Alternative One		Alternative Two	
Positive	Negative	Positive	Negative

Alternative Three		Alternative Four	
Positive	Negative	Positive	Negative

READING 15
INDIVIDUAL FRAMES OF REFERENCE

The other readings have focused on facts, empirical facts. This reading will present experiential facts. Experiential facts express a person's private, often emotional reaction to certain events. Sometimes they are individual and idiosyncratic. Other times, they express shared, but personal, human experience. The following passages present the "experiential facts" of individual reactions to life crises that are frequently encountered by older adults and their families: death of a loved one and placing a parent in a home. These experiential facts can help you understand the person's world view; developing this kind of understanding is vital for the type of counseling you are being trained to do.

The first passage is a letter written by a 62 year old woman whose mother had died and who is approaching the resolution phase of grieving. She wrote this letter in response to a plea from a woman who was despairing over the loss of her husband:

Dear One,

Your letter touched my heart and it quivered. My arms reach out to comfort you.

It's hard. It's painful. I understand. I know. I am there too with you, in a similar circumstance. I too "get stuck" at certain moments in the past and they turn into hours of anguish and despair in the present. I wonder how I can ever help myself . . . how anyone can help . . . if anything can help . . . and if anyone could possibly understand.

I don't know that I can help you. But I can share some of the things I do and try to do and some of the things I am learning.

I too have tried to "bury my grief." That didn't work for me. I found that I have to grieve, that it's really okay and necessary to grieve. And I do — whenever I need to. I also learned, the hard way, that most of the time I have to do it alone. Only with a few people that I take care to select carefully can I let it out. Why? Because I have to grieve in my own way, and at my own times, and for as long as I feel it is necessary for me. Too many of my friends took the "buck up" attitude, or — with a mental patting me on the head attitude of it takes time, you'll get over it. Maybe so, but I have to find that out myself and I got to feeling that those attitudes were patronizing rather than understanding how I really felt and feel.

I too have tried to "keep busy." Sometimes that works, mental and physical work. Sometimes it doesn't help. The extreme busy-ness that I did made me more tired sometimes than the grieving and depression.

What do I do? Different things at different times, depending upon the depth of my grief and depression. I can now do this because I have come, painfully, to learn how deep is deep and how shallow or near the surface my feelings really are.

Sometimes I do nothing; I give in.

Sometimes I give in on purpose, and cry.

Meditation never fails me. When I do not meditate, I usually pay the price by becoming very deeply depressed. Meditation, relaxation, prayer, imagery, call it whatever you want to. If it helps me get myself in touch with myself, it works.

I talk to myself . . . calming talk, confidential talk, reassuring talk. One that never fails me is: I am centered in the peace and calm of God. (And I define God in so many different ways!)

I call up someone, just to hear a human voice.

I walk: in the park, along the streets, downtown, on the beach — however the mood is that day, to see growing things, to see people, to be alone with the vastness of nature and the universe.

I pick at the piano, or listen to my favorite kind of music — favorite for that day. It can range from country western to religious, to electronic modern treatment of the classics.

I wash or take a bath! I find something healing and cleansing in the touch and movement of water. I am too far from a swimming pool to paddle around in.

I read, usually whatever I can get a "lift" from. . . . or sometimes something that is completely new to me and so difficult to understand or figure out that my whole mind must be on it to try to get the point.

I use my hands. Sometimes I dig in the dirt or water the house plants. I get out the oil pastel crayons. I am not an artist. But to move the crayons, to see and use the colors according to my mood, seems satisfying . . . I do not worry about what comes out. Like a child, I just concentrate on the color and trying to do what appeals to me. . . whether I am letting out my emotions or trying to create something I don't let bother me any more. I just lose myself in it. Next to meditation, I find this helps me most when I am the most low. Some people knit, crochet, use their hands and color in other ways. Some weave.

What I am trying to learn: that my ways are best for me and I am trying to find them. I have found two, no three: meditation, color, reading . . . when the going is roughest for me.

I am also trying to learn to be patient with me. Pain is keen. It seems as if it goes on forever, and sometimes I would be through with it, whether in this life or by going on. Then I talk to myself. But I am here, now, on this earth plane. So what have I yet to learn, to do, to be? And I get in a hurry to know and get on with it, whatever it is to be. And I have to say . . slow down, be patient with yourself, take it one moment at a time . . . and know that all moments are not like the deepest, darkest one. And in time, you will know why and what. That's part of my conversation with me. Your conversation will be your own, with yourself.

And I try to let my beloved go, hard as it is. The "experts" say that a part of grieving is "giving permission to die." I prefer to say, giving permission for the other to go on to his or her new experiences. I tend to "hang on." And my mind tells me that is not "good" for either my loved one nor for me. And in time, I will let go. You see, I have come to realize how very much I depended upon my loved one (it was mutual). But now I must learn to depend upon and take care of myself, with whatever help is right for me. Sometimes that help comes through me, my inner self. Sometimes it comes through over people, their words or actions. Sometimes it comes I know not where . . . maybe from the infinite universe, some force that is greater than I am but which I am a part of.

I found very practical and understanding help through talking with a counselor. I also deeply appreciated and saw things in a little different light when I read the beautiful, wise book: FACING DEATH by Robert Kavanaugh. His chapters on grieving and his telling of his own experiences with his family, gave me new knowledge. It also was very comforting. I am sure there are other books too.

I know that no one will take the place of my loved one and I really don't want anyone or thing to do so. That place was special. But there are other places in my life and heart to be filled with their "specials." And I think, really, that they are all important. I shall not try to fill that void. But perhaps the other places will somehow bring about a balance. And maybe I will find that I have a special place to fill too. Right now, I don't know.

If dreams are pleasant, cherish them. If they are not so pleasant, they will clear as your mind clears. At any rate, perhaps they are messages.

If your faith is intact, cherish that. I assume you have one; everyone has. Mine was shaken. I am re-examining my beliefs. Even that is helping, sometimes.

One thing I did not mention above: I found how very much body and mind and emotions are tied together. My doctor found that, for me, a hormone shot now and then helped with the emotions. I know also that when I do not eat properly I get more depressed. I am sure you have talked with your M.D. about depression as well as about your physical heart.

This letter has been too long. You probably received many. But I do care about you and feel with you. And you have helped me by letting me write this to you. Thank you and bless you . . .

Peace . . . . . Love . . .

The following passage was written by a middle-aged daughter who placed her mother in a convalescent hospital after a great deal of internal struggle. The letter is addressed to the director:

My mother spent fifteen of her last seventeen months on this earth in your nursing home. There she died to this earth last May. Since that time I have studied and worked in a project through contacts I made at a university. I have examined more objectively the various experiences I had with your personnel while I shared in the care of my mother. My new knowledge and my thinking lead me to verify the emotional feelings I had at the time: in too many instances both my mother and I were the victims of non-caring and of possible burn out. Let me enumerate.

1. To my knowledge no one ever talked with my mother, even when she mentioned death. She was able to talk intelligently many times; often she was very alert during her last three months. I talked with her about it. But for her to have been able to talk with someone else might have helped her more.

2. I was never told by any one on your staff nor by the medical doctor that she was failing fast, nearing the end.

   Because I was emotionally involved, I probably did not understand the implications of what others were seeing happen to her physical body. If I had been alerted, I would have avoided doing some of the things I did which resulted in a burden of guilt I am now trying to deal with.

3. If your administrative nurse thinks she told me, she must have done it in a manner which I rejected because I felt from her an uncaring attitude.

   I shall never forget the bluntness, and to me, the hardness of her response once during the last three days. I had asked something like, "Can't you do something to ease her?" The reply was, "She is just an old woman." How much more caring would have been, "I am sorry; it is out of our hands." I shall always be disturbed when one human being sees another as a worn out machine. The day of blatant materialism is passing, if it has not already passed. Within the body is a "something" that always knows.

4. On the morning of my mother's last pulse beat, I felt then and still feel that the treatment we received was insensitive and abominable.

Within minutes we were given, to use an old vernacular phrase, the bum's rush. An aide was in the room with a box for the removal of possessions; I wanted to and did do it myself. Mother's body was removed to a cluttered storeroom for the doing of whatever was necessary but I was told to wait for the arrival of the Telophase motor vehicle. Not even the chapel was made available. To me, these actions and rush are indicative of personal and institutionally-spread burn out.

I was fully aware of the fact that my mother's essence had departed, that other patients were in the room, that other persons were waiting the use of the bed space. But I was there. My mind and my spirit were outraged and still are. But I had never been more calm. I knew what I was thinking and feeling. I would not return into a building for "comfort" where no caring or support had been evident. I appreciated their concern; I would have appreciated more their caring and understanding. And I must also say, that those I felt I did receive from the night caretakers, aides and LVN's.

I am aware of your problems as an administrator of a long term care institution for the aged. I believe you are attempting to be modern and innovative. The facility itself shows this in its arrangement, use of color. Have you ever considered decorating the ceilings where the bed-fast focus their attention? or a room for privacy where families may talk, and laugh, or cry and yell together? These would help many patients and families.

Have you ever considered having an active, sensitive, trained person to help patients and families communicate, share feelings, show support? get through the last days here? Many people need such help; I did; I did not get it and I tried. I sought out the medical social work consultant. At that time I wanted help learning to communicate more effectively with my mother. The response was: you can't communicate with the dead. My mother was not dead. Through trial and error I found ways, verbal and non-verbal to communicate. Then, I found a university where my trial and error learnings were validated; they were the same as those being taught to the students there. There I also learned about the Kubler-Ross book. It helped me help myself and my mother. How much time and pain could have been saved. How much more comfort and preparation could have been obtained and given if I had received such supportive service from someone on your staff or the medical doctor. I could write a book — and may — about how I was able, at times, to reach my mother, to reach what your staff said was the unreachable, to get responses, and to know that she was being helped, to prepare herself for her new experience.

QUIZ:

1. What are the main issues of grief involved in the first passage?

2. What has this woman been feeling?

3. Describe this woman's world view.

4. What has helped this woman with her grieving? How is this consistent with her world view?

5. If you were the director of the convalescent hospital, how would this letter make you feel?

6. What difficulties do you think this administrator is faced with in providing adequate services?

7. If you were the director, what changes would you make, if any, in the convalescent hospital?

8. Describe the feelings of the woman who wrote this letter.

READING 16
CASE HISTORIES

Read the following case histories (names are fictitious), and answer the questions which follow. This will help you learn to conceptualize cases, define issues, and develop directions to follow in treatment. Discuss what you write about these cases with your instructor, your supervisor, or your class as a whole. It is important for your growth as a counselor to utilize professional consultants while you work on a case. In many instances, this consultant can be your supervisor. However, you may find yourself working for an agency which does not employ professional clinicians; then you will need to seek out a professional in your community for consultation.

CASE NO. 1

May Smith, a 68-year-old woman, came to the Center because of problems with memory. Her daughter Joan, a 30-year-old interior decorator had contacted the center and made the appointment for her. May's husband, a retired 68-year-old maintenance man, drove her to the center.

During the first interview in which the counselor saw each one alone, May seemed very nervous, quiet, and generally unwilling to communicate with the counselor. When the counselor interviewed the husband separately he complained about May's odd sleeping hours and her cooking. It seemed that May began her cooking preparations too early in the day or too late. She also became confused about which ingredients to put in the food. Sometimes he complained that the food was either too spicy or not spicy enough. When asked if there was anything else that bothered him about his wife, he said that the only thing he could think of was her "anger" and "stubborness," which resulted from his complaints about these things. He did not seem enthusiastic about the prospect of May seeing a counselor. When asked why he had brought May he said it was because Joan had insisted on it.

When Joan was seen by the counselor she was clearly upset. She said that her mother was closed, defensive, "bottled up," and she was worried about her. She added that her mother had always been extremely responsible and bright. In searching for family relationships the counselor concluded that May had seemed to be the backbone of the family. The daughter said that May had finished raising her own brothers and sisters. She worked nights and went to college, married and had a child. Then for many years she was the sole support for the family. Joan said she felt her mother was "suffering a lot," and instead of being open with her family, was defensive and "moody." Joan said that she feared for her mother's "psychological health." Quote: "My mother has changed; she was never like this at all."

QUESTIONS:

1. What kinds of memory evaluation tests should the counselor administer to the client?

2. What are the possible questions the counselor should ask concerning May's physical condition?

3. What family interactions should the counselor note to develop a complete picture of this case?

4. May is the "identified patient" in this case. Should the counselor consider the husband and the daughter as clients also? If so, how would you outline their counseling problems?

5. Study the way May is trying to handle her problem. Do you have any hunches as to why May is taking such a passive, uncooperative attitude in dealing with the memory issue?

6. Do you suspect any other problem aside from a memory loss?

7. If this were your case:

   a. What issues would you deal with?

   b. Would you work with May alone, or would you work also with other members of the family?

c. What resources would you use?

d. What would you see as possible counseling goals?

SUGGESTED TREATMENT APPROACH

1. EVALUATION: When a client has memory complaints it is important to test the client for possible organicity by administering the MSQ and the hand-face test. During the evaluation session it is helpful to take a history of their memory functioning. How long have these complaints existed? What is the nature of their forgetting, i.e. when do they forget? What do they forget? Check for signs of depression. Check for anxiety. Check to see if clients have pressures and crises present in their lives. Also it is helpful to know if the client has moved recently or is being asked to do new and complicated tasks that were previously not asked of them. If they do not do well on the MSQ (miss more that two questions), then they should be referred for a medical examination. If the degree of organicity is severe, they may not be appropriate for counseling for memory problems.

2. EDUCATION: Once the possibility of Brain Syndrome has been ruled out, the counselor may assume that the problem is one of benign forgetting, and can treat the client for that complaint. The counselor can assume with some confidence that the client is worried a great deal about his forgetting and has many misconceptions about what his forgetfulness entails. Therefore, the counselor should attempt to educate him as to what is involved in his forgetting. This will relieve much of his anxiety.
   a. There is a NORMAL benign forgetting in old age for some adults. This does NOT imply senility.
   b. Anxiety, depression, change, and lack of concentration are great contributors to forgetting.
   c. Many individuals, regardless of age, have memory difficulties in some areas (such as forgetting names, numbers, faces).
   d. The more a person valued his memory in the past, the more traumatic his forgetting can be in later years.
   e. His forgetting will not improve unless his anxiety and depression decrease.
   f. There ARE ways the client can behave in order to improve his memory.

3. REDUCING WORRY: The counselor's goals in therapy include education and empathic understanding as necessary first steps in dealing with this kind of problem. Examine the feelings of the client very carefully. Empathic listening and reflection are extremely important. Get a feel for how the client is experiencing his loss, what it means to him, and how anxiety provoking it is.
   The counselor's confidence that the problem can be taken care of is very helpful for the client. Spend time reflecting how others forget. Forgetting plagues all ages and intelligent people at times. Most clients fear that their decrease in memory means a decrease in intelligence.

4. TRAINING FOR BETTER MEMORY: The counselor may want to use some of the memory techniques developed by the Memory Clinic at the University of Southern California. There are other shorter, practical suggestions that the counselor can convey to the client.
   a. Specify exactly what it is that the client wants to remember and can't. Have the client make those things his priorities. Writing down things that are important is extremely helpful.
   b. Have the client "unclutter" his schedule.

114

c. Have the client make a list of priorities and concentrate on accomplishing only those things.

d. Have the client arrange his schedule so that those things which are important for him to remember are attended to first.

e. See if some of the things that are forgotten can be more easily remembered by arranging for a more specific set of memory materials:

   (1) more clocks around

   (2) calendars in each room

   (3) road maps and street maps in the car

   (4) a large list of daily events

   (5) phone numbers written in several places

5. FAMILY DYNAMICS: Very often a forgetting problem is complicated by the family's reaction to the client's forgetting. Check out how the various family members react to the forgetting and the kinds of messages they convey to the client.

6. CHECK THE CLIENT'S PAST FUNCTIONING IN THE AREA OF INTELLIGENCE AND MEMORY: Many times clients who panic over benign memory problems have a history of excellent memory and above average intellectual functioning. The decrease in this area arouses panic and fears of senility.

7. CHECK FOR MORE SEVERE PROBLEMS: Often clients who are concerned about memory loss and come to the counselor with memory as the presenting problem have emotional and/or relationship problems, and memory loss is a side effect of those problems. The most common underlying problems seen are: depression, anxiety, marital problems, self-concept problems, worry and concern about aging or tension stemming from one or more crises.

8. CHECK FOR ILLNESS AND MEDICATION: There may be physical ailments which are painful or debilitating and cause a client to concentrate more on them than on what they are doing. Medications for some diseases make clients drowsy, disoriented, and/or interfere with attention and concentration.

CASE NO. 2

William Garret, a forty-two year old businessman came to see a counselor because he was upset about his mother. Mrs. Garret was an 82 year old woman who had been widowed for a year. William told the counselor that he had lived with his parents his entire life and although there had been problems, he had been fairly happy until recently. His father, the president of a small company had died suddenly the previous year. He felt his father's death seemed to have quite an impact upon his mother, even though she had always claimed to dislike the man. "Even though she said my Dad was cold and more interested in the Company than in her, she talks about him quite a bit and from what she says you'd think it had been an ideal marriage." "My Mother used to say that I was much more loving than my Dad and she did spoil me quite a bit. This made trouble I think, between my Dad and me and I think for most of my life he resented me. As I got older, I felt bad about this, and for the last few years of his life, my Dad and I began to get along. I'd say, when he died, we were pretty good friends." William was worried and upset about his mother's present behavior. According to William, his mother had begun acting "strange" even before his father died. She had become increasingly forgetful and sometimes left things in the oven an entire day. "When I return from work and find things all mixed up, she denies she had anything to do with it and becomes very defensive, or gives me some kind of crazy explanation. She's not always like this, but it still keeps me worried." William said that he had been going with a woman Irene for nearly three years. He said that he really loved Irene and wanted to marry her.

William related that a few months previously, Irene had given him an ultimatum. If he didn't marry her within six months, she would move back East. "My mother can't stand Irene, and gives me hell when I go out with her." William said he wanted to marry Irene but Irene said that if they got married, it would be "out of the question" to have his mother live with them. He said he was afraid to leave his mother alone for too long. When he suggested a retirement facility to his mother, she went into a rage. "She accused me of leaving her to die alone in a prison."

Within the last few months William reported that he had begun to change. He wasn't sleeping well, he had lost interest in his work and even his sex life which had been quite satisfactory with Irene was suffering. "I feel miserable most of the time. Often I feel anguished. It's as if nothing matters and yet, I've got all this responsibility that I carry around with me. Irene suggested I come to see you. I didn't come for awhile, but then when I began to feel really low. I got scared. It's not that I really want to kill myself or would, but what scares me is that it pops into my mind a lot. Basically I feel stuck. If my Dad were alive, he'd be able to handle Mom. Now it's all on me, and the way I feel now, I can't handle a thing.

QUIZ:

1. Define the problem(s) presented in this case.

2. What are some of the issues involved?

3. What is Mr. Garrett feeling?

4. His resulting physical and emotional symptoms are common to a frequent clinical problem seen in older adults. What is it?

5. What counseling goals might you develop with Mr. Garrett?

6. What do you see as his alternatives?

Providing Closure   9

"Providing Closure" means ending the counseling relationship. When the counseling goals have been achieved, the counseling relationship ends. Some counseling relationships are short-lived. Many clients have simple, unidimensional problems they wish to explore. Once they explore their problem, they make a decision and do not return for further counseling. It is not unknown for clients to receive the help they require in one session. However most counseling relationships last for many sessions. The rapport between counselor and client increases with time. Much has been written about the value of good client-counselor rapport. Some theorists believe that the "curative" aspect in counseling has as much or more to do with the quality of the relationship than with the method and tools used by the counselor. Robert Carkhuff once implied that if the world were filled with people who were truly human, counselors and people in the helping professions would be out of jobs. Counselors often hear from clients that it was their caring, their empathy and their personal qualities which made the client feel better about himself and his life. Ending the counseling relationship is not the same as ending a business partnership. The client has let you into his most personal world. It is for that reason that you are a special person to him. Hopefully, he is also special to you. In this chapter, we will give you some suggestions on ending the relationship. These are only suggestions. We suspect that you will have a personal style for accomplishing closure that will be far more effective than anything we can suggest.

EXERCISE ONE:

The group will read Parts One and Two in the following readings. When everyone has finished reading, the group will discuss what has been read with the group leader.

PART I: MAKING A DECISION

Once the counselor and the client have examined the possible alternatives and their positive and negative consequences, a decision is usually made. The making of the decision is sometimes very difficult for the client because what becomes apparent in exploring alternatives is the fact that there is usually no decision which does not carry with it negative consequences. For example, the young mother in our example in Chapter Eight finally decided to go back to college and earn a Master's degree. She was aware, however, when she made her decision, that she would also have to adjust to the negative aspects of her choice. Her leisure time would be reduced; she would have to budget her time and money very carefully; and she would have to find a way to spend enough time with her children to reduce her feelings of guilt. She chose to endure the negative consequences of her decision to return to school because the rewards of such a decision were worth it to her. This is precisely what is involved in making difficult decisions, a weighing and balancing of pain and reward.

The responsibility of the counselor in this process is one of helping the client see clearly all pertinent aspects of his problem as well as alternatives. It is also to encourage the client to be honest about his true feelings and motivations, to understand himself at deeper and deeper levels. When this is accomplished, the counselor waits patiently while the client decides what to do with his life. This is the key concept in the art of counseling. The client is the one to make the final decision because it is HIS problem, HIS choice and HIS life. When the client makes a choice, the counselor should respect his choice even if he believes the choice is unwise. The choice is always wise in context of the client's world-view. This of course excludes choices which would result in some form of physical destruction. But fortunately such choices are rare.

Sometimes clients choose to make no decision. They are ambivalent and sometimes fearful. They prefer to remain in a holding pattern rather than make any changes in their lives. Choosing not to chose, is also a choice and should be respected as such. If you as a counselor work several weeks or even months with a client who ultimately chooses to do nothing about his life, you should not feel as if you have failed him. The purpose of counseling is not to change people or their lives but rather to give them clarity, understanding, and insight into themselves and their situations. This, in itself, always helps the client in some way. If clients who come to you for counseling do in fact make significant changes that make them happier, then that is indeed a bonus.

PART II: PROVIDING CLOSURE.

The logical time to terminate the counseling relationship is when the counseling goal has been accomplished. It may happen that while exploring one problem several more emerge. The client may wish to continue the counseling relationship in order to explore the other problems. If the counselor feels that this is beneficial and if he himself wishes to continue, then new goals are defined and the relationship continues.

If it happens that the counseling goals are accomplished and both client and counselor agree to terminate the relationship, then the counseling moves on to the last stage which we refer to as Closure.

HOW TO END THE COUNSELING RELATIONSHIP

1. TIE UP LOOSE ENDS: If there is any unfinished business between you and your client, try to take care of it before terminating the relationship. "Unfinished business" in this sense refers to unresolved feelings between yourself and the counselee.

2. TIME IT WISELY: Because the relationship between a counselor and client is usually very intimate for the client, ending the relationship may be difficult for him. When his problem is resolved, you may wish to terminate the relationship and open your schedule for another client. While this makes good sense from your point of view, it may seem

cold and uncaring to the client. Therefore it is important that you be sensitive to the feelings of the client about ending the relationship. If you see the end coming, bring it up in a session and work any difficulties through with the client. If you and the client mutually decide to end the relationship, invite him back for an additional session if you wish. This is another way in which you can be sure that all business between the two of you is settled.

3. THE GRIEF OF GOOD-BYE: Ending a close relationship always involves a sense of loss, a kind of grieving. Both you and your client need to explore the feelings that can come with such a loss: anger, sadness, guilt, fear of abandonment, excitement at starting on a new course. These feelings can be discussed openly. One issue that may arise at this point is the client's feeling that there is no one else with whom to talk as intimately as with the counselor. If this is so, counselor and client may decide to spend a few more sessions working toward a goal of helping the client to develop a supportive network of friends and at least one confidant.

4. REFER WHEN NECESSARY: When you have gone as far with a client as is necessary to accomplish the counseling goal, but not far enough to give him complete service, then you may wish to refer him to a place or person who can give him more specific help. For example, if a woman decides that she can no longer care for her ailing mother, you may wish to refer her to an agency which can help her find a suitable care facility. You may at times have a client whose problems are so severe that you feel inadequate to deal with them. You should then refer that client to a skilled clinician for more in-depth treatment.

5. UNFINISHED ENDINGS: Your clients will not always come in for a final session. You will probably have at least one client who just stops coming to appointments and whom you cannot reach by phone or letter. This leaves you to deal with the grieving process alone. We suggest you talk to your supervisors about how this loss makes you feel.

6. AN INVITATION: Under optimal conditions, when clients leave therapy, they have the resources and confidence with which to deal with any new problems that may arise. Yet, they may still want you and your agency to be part of their support system. It often makes them feel more comfortable and confident when you invite them to call you and/or your agency if there is anything they would like to talk about in the future.

7. FOLLOW-UP: After you have terminated a client, it is a thoughtful gesture to contact him sometime later to see how he is doing. This thoughtfulness on your part is an indication of your caring, and clients seem especially appreciative when you do this.

EXERCISE TWO: PRACTICING CLOSURE.

The training program we have outlined in this manual is one which has involved much self-reflection and self-revelation. Throughout the exercises you have learned much about yourself and your fellow group members. It is impossible to be involved in a program such as this without experiencing a sense of personal growth and a sense of union with your group and your group leader. In this chapter we have dealt with the issue of closure with your prospective clients. The purpose of this exercise is to provide an opportunity for you and your group to begin to enact some type of closure with one another. Providing closure entails tying up loose ends, discussing feelings with one another about the program and your participation in it. The following are some discussion questions which you may wish to use as an outline for your discussion. Because providing closure is very often a question of personal style, it is possible that members of the group will have other creative suggestions of how to utilize this time and provide a sense of group closure for the training program.

SUGGESTED QUESTIONS FOR DISCUSSION

1. What have you learned about yourself during the training?

2. How do you feel about the training? about yourself as a future counselor? about working with this group?

3. Is there anything in the way of "unfinished business" you would like to finish with another member of the group? the group as a whole? the group leader?

4. What do you believe are your personal qualities which will aid you to be a good counselor?

5. What do you believe you will have to work on in order to be a better counselor?

6. As you look around at the members of your group, is there anyone you would like to share something personal with?

7. Are there any members of the group whom you feel have personal qualities which you believe will aid them to become excellent counselors?

8. Are there any members of the group whom you would like to make a suggestion on a quality of theirs which they might consider improving in order to make themselves a better counselor?

9. Do you have any doubts or fears about yourself as a future counselor that you would like to share with the group?

10. Why do you want to be a counselor?

EXERCISE THREE: PREPARING FOR PRACTICUM.

A PRACTICUM is an actual counseling session in which trainees experience counseling under supervision. The next and last training session will consist of you doing actual counseling as well as being counseled yourself. In the next session you will have an opportunity to counsel a fellow group member with a personal problem. You will also be asked to bring to the session an actual problem in your life and one of your fellow group members will be your counselor and will attempt to use the training lessons in order to help you with your problem. For homework, examine your life and decide which issue you would like help dealing with. When you return for your last session, be prepared to explain your problem to your counselor. The problem should be one which is immediate and personal. We advise against using simulated problems because such kinds of problems are difficult for counselors to work with. If you are having difficulty identifying a problem which might be used in the next session, discuss this difficulty with the group and group leader. This difficulty, itself, might be the problem you want to discuss.

READING 17
WHEN TO GET HELP

Sometimes your clients will need a different kind of help than you can give them. This will be fairly obvious when they need legal or medical assistance. However, it is more difficult in the case of psychological problems. There are several indications that someone should see a psychotherapist (clinical psychologist or psychiatrist) rather than a counselor. When you see the following indications, we recommend that you refer the client to your supervisor, a clinical psychologist, or a psychiatrist for a review of the case:

1. Past history of hospitalization for psychological problems.

2. DELUSIONS: a false belief about oneself, such as delusions of grandeur and delusions of persecution.

3. HALLUCINATIONS: Seeing, hearing, feeling, tasting, smelling something that does not exist.

4. Suicide threats.

5. Depression and withdrawal to the point where the person no longer eats or sleeps.

6. Threats of violence.

There are laws and ethical standards regarding confidentiality. They may change from state to state, so check those for the state within which you are practicing. Commonly, you cannot reveal any information about your client, including the fact that the person IS your client, without the client's written or oral permission. This does not apply to your clinical supervision. Sometimes, there are exceptions made for consultations between professionals working for the same client and/or within the same agency. Usually, exceptions to these laws are cases where persons are in imminent danger of harming themselves or others.

QUIZ:

1. What is a delusion?

2. Name three indications that you should refer your client to your supervisor, clinical psychologist, or psychiatrist.

3. What are the laws and ethical standards regarding confidentiality in your state?

READING 18
IMPORTANCE OF REFERRALS

Older clients often need help from other service agencies. They may need information about social security, internists who specialize in geriatrics, dental work, retirement homes, and legal services. If the agency you are working for does not have a listing of these services for older individuals, try to find an agency in your community which does.

The following is the general procedure for referring a client to other services:

1. Locate one or several agencies which provide these services.

2. You or the client call and make an appointment with that agency.

3. Afterwards, call both the agency and the client to see how the referral went.

These procedures can help protect the client from being passed around from one agency to another.

If the services are relevant to your counseling (such as a physical examination), you will probably want to exchange information with the other agency. To do this legally in California, you need the written or oral consent of your client. A written request for release of information signed and dated by your client is usually the safest, more convenient way. Then, after the initial referral, you can write a letter to the other agency requesting the needed information and include your client's release. You will get the best replies if your letter is specific, listing the questions you would like answered. The following are questions you might want to include:

To an internist (geriatrician):

1. Are there any physical problems which might contribute to this man's impotence?

2. If any medication needs to be prescribed for this patient, please let me know if it will interfere with his functioning, such as possible dizziness or confusion.

3. Please rule out the possibility of an infection.

4. This patient complains of digestive problems and constipation. Are there any medical explanations for these problems?

5. The psychological testing done at our clinic indicated that this patient's memory problems may be due to an acute problem such as overmedication, tumor, endocrine imbalance, malnutrition, or local infection. Please rule out these possibilities.

6. I would appreciate a report on any physical problems which might be affecting psychological functioning.

To a psychiatrist:

1. This patient appears to be depressed. Please review for appropriate medication.

2. What is your diagnosis?

3. Would you recommend hospitalization?

4. What are your suggestions for treatment of this patient at our clinic. (Describe the resources available in your clinic.)

5. Please review this patient's medication. Could this medication be contributing to this patient's depression (or confusion)?

6. I am referring this patient for a Psychiatric Evaluation. Please send me a copy of your report.

To a Clinical Psychologist:

1. What is your diagnosis of this client?

2. What are your recommendations for treatment of this client?

3. What is your assessment of this client's intellectual capacity?

4. What is your assessment of this client's competency?

5. Does your testing rule out chronic brain syndrome?

6. What is your assessment of the dynamics of this client's personality?

7. Please send me a copy of your psychological evaluation.

8. Is this client psychotic?

9. We feel this client may be too severely disturbed for treatment at our clinic. Can you recommend psychotherapists and/or mental health facilities that will be better able to help him/her?

To an attorney:

1. The family of this client wish to have a competency hearing. My client needs to be represented at the hearing. How can our clinic help you with the case?

2. The clinical psychologist (or psychiatrist) at our clinic has evaluated this client's competency. Would you like a copy of that report?

HOMEWORK:

Call the information and referral agencies in your area and get a list of specialists in gerontology or practitioners willing to work with older individuals. Get their phone numbers.

A.   M.D.'s

Internists

    1.   phone:

    2.   phone:

    3.   phone:

Neurologists

    1.   phone:

    2.   phone:

Opthalmologists

    1.   phone:

    2.   phone:

Psychiatrists

    1.   phone:

    2.   phone:

B.   Clinical Psychologists

    1.   phone:

    2.   phone:

C.   Social Workers

    1.   phone:

    2.   phone:

D. Dentists

    1.   phone:

    2.   phone:

E. Lawyers

    1.   phone:

    2.   phone:

F. Hot-lines or Suicide Prevention Centers

    1.   phone:

    2.   phone:

Also, look up the phone numbers of the following resources:

A. Community centers providing services to the elderly:

    1.   phone:

    2.   phone:

B. Nutrition Programs

    1.   phone:

    2.   phone:

C. Social Security

    1. Main Office   phone:

    2. Medicare   phone:

D. Legal Aid   phone:

E. Universities and colleges with gerontology programs:

    1.   phone:

    2.   phone:

F. Information and Referral Agencies:

    1.   phone:

    2.   phone:

Practicum

10

The Practicum period provides counselors an opportunity to begin counseling under supervision and direction. There are many ways to conduct practicums. The following exercise presents a few variations of methods which have been found to be useful.

DIRECTIONS FOR EXERCISE ONE:

Read over the various methods of conducting practicums and decide which method or combination of methods you prefer.

1. FISHBOWL: A practicum done in a fishbowl is one in which two members of the group, one playing the role of the counselor, the other playing the role of the counselee, are seated in the middle of the room. The remainder of the group are seated in a circle surrounding the group. The dyad in the center begin the counseling session, and the members observe and critique the session. After about twenty minutes have passed, the members consisting of the counselor and counselee end the session. The group leader and members give feedback to the counselor concerning how they observed the session.

2. DYADS: The group divides into groups of two. Each group of two finds a spot away from the other members to conduct a counseling session. One member of the dyad plays the part of the counselee for forty minutes while the other plays the part of the counselor. After the forty minutes are up the two members discuss and critique the session for fifteen minutes. The roles are then reversed, and the session is done again. Discussion and critique are again repeated after the session ends. During this time the group leader circulates and observes all of the sessions, moving from dyad to dyad until he has observed each session. At the end of the exercise the entire group meets to discuss what they have learned from the exercise.

3. TRIADS: The group divides itself into three groups consisting of three members apiece. One member is the counselee; another member is the counselor; and the third member is the observer. Each member plays one of the various roles for twenty minutes apiece, rotating roles until all have had the opportunity to counsel, observe and be counseled. The observer member makes notes on the sessions and gives feedback to the counselee and counselor after each counseling session. The group leader circulates and observes every group. At the end of the exercise the entire group meets together and discusses the exercise.

EXERCISE TWO: CRITIQUING SESSIONS

A method of critiquing sessions which we have found helpful is for each observer-member to jot down on a piece of paper, things which impressed them about the session. The feedback session is intended to provide counselors with constructive criticism which will enable them to improve their counseling skills. Some points to keep in mind while noting criticisms and expressing those criticisms to the counselors are:

* Most counselors will feel a bit nervous and self-conscious during their first public counseling session. It is understood that this inescapable anxiety will interfere somewhat with the effectiveness of the counselor's performance. Therefore, all members should automatically make allowances for some hesitancy on the part of the new counselor. It is helpful during the feedback session to discuss with the counselor his feelings and let him express to the group his feelings concerning his counseling in public.

* Feedback should consist of constructive criticism. Constructive criticism consists of both positive and negative feedback. Positive feedback contains all comments concerning the counselor's performance which the observers found to be facilitative and helpful to the client. Negative feedback should be specific. a) If the counselor has missed an important issue which the counselee would have found helpful to develop, then the observers should note the missing issue and suggest to the counselor that it would have been facilitative to pursue that issue. b) If the counselor used Level I responses, then those responses should be noted specifically and expressed to the counselor. c) If an observer has comments concerning the non-verbal behavior of the counselor or counselee, then those behaviors should be noted and expressed. d) Any other important issues which arose during the session which an observer wishes to comment upon should be stated and explained.

* Feedback should be helpful and encouraging for the beginning counselor. It should be: a) constructive b) given in very specific terms, backed up by an example taken from the counseling session c) should consist of behaviors which the observer found helpful as well as some suggestions for improvement d) all criticisms both positive and negative should be given in such a manner that the counselor may ask for clarification and express his feelings about the various feedbacks given him.

* If any member is not satisfied with the feedback that he received, then it becomes a group issue. The class should not terminate until that issue is settled as satisfactorily as possible under the circumstances of time and structure which is always rather limited under such a training program. If time does not permit a satisfactory conclusion of a problem, some arrangement should be made to help the counselor achieve closure, even if that has to be done at a later time.

One last remark concerning practicum sessions. Some institutions, such as university Counseling Departments, have facilities which contain rooms which are equipped with mirrors and sound equipment which enable observers to watch counseling sessions in a room other than that in which the counseling is taking place. If the trainers can utilize this kind of arrangement for the practicum session, then we strongly advise that they do so. We have found the use of these rooms extremely helpful for counselors and observers alike.

READING 19
REVIEW OF INFORMATION

This is a lecture which you can read or your instructor can present in class:

When working with older clients it is important to understand certain aspects of adult development and aging and to be aware of specific clinical problems which can occur in old age. To begin with, there are many myths about old age which could give a counselor a negative attitude about working with older clients. Most of these myths have been refuted by recent research in the areas of learning, intelligence, and aging. For example, it is important for a gerontological counselor to know that older clients can learn and change. There are some decrements in sensory acuity and speed of learning; however, they are rarely severe enough to impair an older person's ability to function competently in the world. When impairments are so severe, they are usually due to disease and not normal aging. Since behavior generally slows with age, older individuals usually function better in situations without excessive time limits, and they learn better when they are not rushed. It is a fallacy to think that all people lose their memories when they get old. Most older individuals function within the normal range of intellectual and memory functioning.

Another myth is that older people do not benefit from psychotherapy. Freud did a lot to perpetuate this myth. However, several analysts have tested this belief — including Martin Grotjan — and found it to be false because psychoanalysis was successful with their patients. In fact, Jung felt the most important work in therapy could only be done with middle-aged and older adults.

By entering the field of counseling older adults, you will provide services where they are very needed — and possible to give — because many professionals, still holding onto old myths, shy away from this field.

When counseling an older adult or his/her family, you will often find that the problems which are raised are problems related to aging. Often these problems become extremely painful to the client because the client is misinformed. This is why the counselor should be familiar with common misconceptions concerning aging and be prepared to correct them. One problem concerns the question of placing parents in a retirement home. On the other hand, a son or daughter may come to you for help because he or she wants to make it more comfortable for an older parent to live at home. It is not uncommon to find that middle-aged children have not consulted with their older parents when they were making decisions that concern them. This can teach the parent to act in dependent, childlike ways when they could be functioning as mature adults. It can also make the parents very angry and disrupt an otherwise good relationship between them and their children. It is helpful to discuss having a family conference which includes the parents. In this way the parents' needs and wants are taken into consideration, and they can probably make the most appropriate decision themselves.

If the older person decides to remain in his home, there are many ways to compensate for some physical losses, thereby making his environment more comfortable.

1. Visual acuity can be aided by:
   a. High illumination without glare;
   b. Short periods of exposure;
   c. Enlarged figures;
   d. Figures that contrast greatly with their background.

2. Auditory acuity can be aided by mechanical devices on telephones which increase the volume in the receiver.

3. Avoidance of situations involving time pressures can compensate for the slowing of behavior.

4. Chairs with arms on them make it easier for older adults to rise and seat themselves.

5. Activities available for the older individual which he finds enjoyable can be helpful. It can make a big difference to some older individual to engage in activities which help keep the household going because it is important to some people to feel they are making worthwhile contributions.

6. Oftentimes when an older person wants to live alone in his/her own home, but can no longer take care of it adequately, part-time outside help can aid in allowing the individual to remain autonomous. Such outside help can include a housekeeper or meals-on-wheels.

Many older adults will come to you with memory complaints. Current research is indicating that memory complaints are more often signs of depression than of actual memory loss. In fact, when many clients with memory complaints are given memory tests, they perform well on them. Therefore, when a client comes to you complaining about his memory, it is important to look for signs of depression — which I will discuss later — emotional stress, or preoccupation with problems. Recent memory loss can occur when the older person is blocking painful present memories in favor of past memories which are either more pleasant or which the person has idealized (Butler, 1973).

There are several good diagnostic tools which can be used to distinguish memory complaints from actual memory loss due to organic brain syndrome. Sometimes organic brain syndrome is called "senility" or "senile dementia." It is a disease, and it is not caused by normal aging. These diagnostic tools also help distinguish between two types of brain syndrome — chronic and acute. This is an important distinction because we know how to effectively treat acute brain syndrome whereas we only know how to slow the deterioration that comes with chronic brain syndrome. Before going on to looking at these diagnostic tools, I would like to tell you a little more about organic brain syndrome. Brain syndrome is a disease which severely impairs cognitive functioning; this impairment is especially obvious in memory. It can also result in little or no emotional response or excessive emotional responses — such as laughing or yelling at inappropriate times. As a result, the patient can have impaired judgment and look disoriented; however, these are also symptoms of other, more readily treatable problems.

Chronic brain syndrome refers to clinical cases where brain dysfunction is irreversible by our present methods. It is usually caused by vascular problems, such as circulatory problems in the brain or strokes, or by brain diseases which result in the death of brain cells or the tangling up of the connections between brain cells (neuro-fibrillary tangles). There are many questions that have yet to be answered about chronic brain syndrome: Is it caused by a virus? Is it a genetic defect because it tends to run in families? Is it influenced by education and exercise? Clinical observations suggest that better educated individuals function more adequately than less well educated individuals with the same severity of brain syndrome.

Acute brain syndrome is reversible. It can be caused by malnutrition, infections (including kidney and bladder), and drug side effects. Acute brain syndrome has a more sudden onset than chronic does. Also, when a client has acute brain syndrome, he will often give evidence of denial or delusions when talking to you.

Let us turn now to the diagnostic tools. In your workbook you will find a copy of the Mental Status Questionnaire, often called the MSQ, and the Face-Hand Test. Let us begin with the MSQ. It is suggested that you introduce the MSQ by asking the question: "What is your main problem? Why did you come here?" Clients with acute brain syndrome will often give a metaphorical answer to this question. Then you can introduce the MSQ in a way you are comfortable with. One way is to tell the client you want to ask them a few questions to see how well they are remembering things.

What is your Main Problem? Why did you Come Here?

MENTAL STATUS QUESTIONNAIRE

(from Kahn, R. L., *et al.* Brief objective measures for the determination of mental status in the aged. *American Journal of Psychiatry, 117:* 326-328, 1960.)

1. Where are you now? (What place is this? What is the name of this place? What kind of place is it? These questions are asked, if necessary).

2. Where is it located? (address, approximately)

3. What is the date today? Day?

4. Month?

5. Year?

6. How old are you?

7. When were you born? Month?

8. Year of birth?

9. Who is the president of the United States?

10. Who was president before him?

Additional questions —

1. Have you ever been in another (place with same name)?

2. Who am I?

3. What do I do (what is my job called?)

4. Have you ever seen me before?

5. Where were you last night?

6. What medication are you on?

7. When did you start having problems with your memory?

This test is scored by the number of errors a person makes.

0 to 2 errors means none or minimal brain syndrome.
3 to 5 errors mean mild to moderate brain syndrome.
6 to 8 errors mean at least moderate brain syndrome.
9 to 10 errors mean severe organic brain syndrome.

Of course, this is a valid test only if the patient is not too deaf to hear you and there is no real language difficulty, and the patient is not antagonistic and resisting testing purposely.

When acute brain syndrome is present you will often get unusual answers to question number one. He might say that your clinic is a repair shop or a cemetery.

It is important to note here some specific symptoms of emotional problems which sometimes lead to a MISdiagnosis of brain syndrome.

1. poor attention;

2. poor concentration;

3. preoccupation with somatic symptoms.

4. hypochondriasis;

5. fear of death;

6. feeling depressed, lonely, bored, or rejected;

7. anger directed at themselves, their children, or the world.

Also, some doctors MISdiagnose brain syndrome. Arteriosclerosis in the eye is NOT diagnostic of arteriosclerosis in the brain.

To reiterate and emphasize, it is important to diagnose brain syndrome carefully. Too often, older people have been labelled "senile" and left without treatment because of MISdiagnoses.

How do you feel about talking about sex with your older clients? If you had an older couple for marriage counseling, would you ask them about their sexual relationship? Sex is another area where there are many myths, even outside the area of aging. Let us review with you some facts about sex and aging.

1. Sex can be an enjoyable experience for most older adults. It is normal for both man and woman to have orgasms.

2. When sex is not enjoyable — and the older person, and/or the person's partner, consider this a problem — sex can become more enjoyable through medical and psychological treatment. Please refer to Masters and Johnson's HUMAN SEXUAL INADEQUACY as a resource for such treatment.

3. There is a higher incidence of heart attacks in older adults. This need not interfere greatly with a satisfying sexual relationship. After a person recovers from the crisis of a heart attack, sexual intercourse does not endanger his health.

4. It takes longer for a man over 50 to get an erection.

5. The older male usually needs more tactile stimulation to get an erection. Visually arousing material usually does not excite an older man as much as it excites a younger man.

6. It takes an older man a longer time to have a climax than it does a younger man.

7. There is a higher incidence of psychological impotence in men over 50.

8. The clinician should check for the following causes of impotence in older clients:
   a. certain drugs (especially for hypertension);
   b. boredom with sexual partner;
   c. not enough tactile stimulation;
   d. disease (for example, diabetes);
   e. fear of old age and/or the belief that old age must bring impotence;
   f. excessive use of alcohol.

9. After menopause, the lining of a woman's vagina may become drier and more delicate. This can make sexual intercourse painful. This problem can be treated by using additional lubrication or appropriate medication.

There are two more facts which can be useful when you begin counseling older adults. (1) There is an increased incidence of depression in old age; and (2) there is a high incidence of suicide in old age, particularly in white males. There are several signs which can alert the counselor to the possibility of depression:

1. feelings of guilt;

2. feelings of unworthiness;

3. loneliness;

4. boredom;

5. constipation or diarrhea;

6. sexual disinterest;

7. impotence;

8. fatigue;

9. insomnia or change in sleep patterns;

10. somatic complaints.

Since there is a high incidence of suicide in old age, it is important to know what signs may indicate a possible suicide. First of all, all suicide threats should be taken seriously when they occur, especially when the person knows how and when they plan to commit suicide. However, older people often kill themselves without making a plea for help through a suicide threat. Therefore, the following list can be useful in identifying clients who might be suicidal:

1. depression;

2. withdrawal;

3. bereavement;

4. isolation — someone who is widowed or single;

5. expectation of death from some cause;

6. indicted helplessness or feeling helpless;

7. institutionalization;

8. physical illness;

9. desire and a rational decision to protect survivors from financial disaster;

10. philosophical decision that there is no more pleasure or purpose in life;

11. meaninglessness of life;

12. decreased self-regard;

13. organic mental deterioration;

14. changes in sleep patterns — nightmares.

This has been a quick review of some of the facts about aging which are important for you to know when you are counseling older adults. At this point, please refer to the books on the reference list for more complete and comprehensive coverage of the psychology of aging and clinical gerontology. Even though this review is not complete, it covers a great deal of information in a condensed fashion. Therefore, you may want to ask your trainers to expand on this information.

HOMEWORK:

Your homework is to "gerontologize" someone you know. TO GERONTOLOGIZE means to teach someone the basic facts on aging. There are a variety of ways you could do this. For example, you could share with a friend the most interesting and/or personally relevant facts you have learned about aging. Another way is to give a lecture or lead a discussion group on one of the subject areas you have read.

READING 20
THE FINAL TEST

ANSWER THE FOLLOWING QUESTIONS WITH A **T** IF THE ANSWER IS **TRUE** OR WITH AN **F** IF THE ANSWER IS **FALSE**.

1. There is a general slowing of behavior with advancing age_____.

2. Old dogs can't learn new tricks_____.

3. All older individuals eventually become senile_____.

4. There is no way to really know if someone has brain syndrome _____.

5. Generally, it takes longer for a man over 50 to get an erection_____.

6. There is an increased incidence of depression in old age_____.

7. Children should keep their older parents in their houses as long as possible _____.

8. With the process of normal aging, all senses tend to become duller after age 70 _____.

9. After menopause, intercourse can be painful for a woman_____.

10. Sexual behavior can be influenced greatly by social and religious values and beliefs about sex and old age_____.

11. Sexual problems can be treated medically and psychologically_____.

12. Arteriosclerosis in the eye is a good indication that there is hardening of the arteries in the brain_____.

13. The older man needs the same amount of stimulation to get an erection as a young man does_____.

14. Generally, personality characteristics remain stable across the life span_____.

15. In older individuals, any intellectual decline due to normal aging is usually too small to interfere with their ability to function adequately in the world_____.

16. Night driving is more difficult for some older individuals_____.

17. Some prescribed medication can interfere with thinking and memory_____.

18. After a person recovers from the crisis of a heart attack, sexual intercourse does not endanger his health_____.

19. When someone is very depressed, he or she may often contemplate suicide _____ .

20. Depression or other emotional problems can be confused with brain syndrome _____.

21. After age 20, intelligence declines _____.

22. Chronic brain syndrome is always severe _____ .

23. In general, it takes an older man longer to climax than it does a younger man _____ .

24. It is abnormal behavior for an older person to keep talking about the past _____.

25. Old people cannot learn _____.

26. Perceptual impairments, with normal aging, are usually so severe that they make it hard for the older person to function adequately in the world _____.

27. The highest incidence of suicide is in white males over the age of 65 _____ .

28. Suicide threats should not be taken seriously _____.

29. Barbiturates may make an older person anxious _____ .

30. Older persons generally do not have orgasms _____.

31. There is a higher incidence of impotence in older men _____.

32. Older individuals can withstand as much stress as younger individuals _____.

33. Drugs can increase memory powers _____.

34. As individuals get older (past sixty), they sometimes engage in fewer activities because they do things more slowly _____.

35. Personality types are categories which are used to identify particular sets of behaviors typically exhibited by some people _____.

PART II — Write out the answers to the following questions:

36. How can you make it easier for someone to become familiar with new living situations?

37. What can cause a marked decline in an individual's intellectual functioning?

139

38. Acute brain syndrome refers to cases where the symptoms are:

39. These are symptoms which may occur with what disorder?
    a. impairment of memory;
    b. disorientation as to time and/or place;
    c. lack of concern about problems or, possibly, sudden unexplained shifts in behavior or mood;
    d. impairment of intellectual functioning.

40. Chronic brain syndrome refers to clinical cases where brain dysfunction is

41. The three main determinants of personality which are most commonly studied are

    _____ , _____ , and

    _____ .

42. What are the optimal conditions which aid visual perception in the elderly?

43. In older individuals, tranquilizers may interfere with_____and

    cause_____ .

44. Life review might be used to resolve the conflict which Erickson presents as the major problem besetting older adults. This conflict is _____

    versus_____ .

45. The four stages of grief are

46. Briefly, describe how you might use one of the developmental theories of personality when working with an older client.

Appendix A

ANSWERS TO QUIZZES

READING 1

Answers to the Quiz:

1. Slowing.

2. Throw off his/her timing.
   Limit activities.

3. Depression.
   Time pressures.
   Many activities to be done at once.

4. Remove self from time-pressured situations.
   Take on fewer activities.

READING 2

Answer to the Quiz:

1. Age 70

2. a. Loss of hearing more often occurs with high tones.
   b. Men usually have greater hearing losses than women.

3. a. High illumination without glare.
   b. Short periods of exposure.
   c. Enlarge figures.
   d. Figures that contrast greatly with their background.

4.

READING 3

Answers to the quiz:

1. Yes, older individuals can learn new information and new skills.

2. On learning tasks, the PERFORMANCE of older adults is poorer than that of young adults.

3. This training manual has tried to utilize these principles.

READING 4

Asnwers to the Quiz:

1. originally: ability to succeed in a traditional classroom situation.
   possibly: intellectual capacity.

2. Young adulthood through late middle-age.

3. a. Using old materials in new ways.
   b. Using new materials in old ways.
   c. Using new materials in new ways.

4. Medical and/or psychological problems.

READING 5

Answers to the Quiz:

1. SENILITY is a disease process; SENESCENCE is normal aging.

2. BENIGN forgetfulness is the forgetting of only the details of a recent event whereas MALIGNANT forgetfulness is forgetting the event itself.

3. a. Memory loss
   b. Recent events may be painful
   c. Past memories may be idealized or more pleasant

4. With depression, there are more complaints of poor memory, but there is usually no real memory loss.

5. No, there are no drugs which enhance memory — only drugs which can impair it.

READING 6

Answers to the Quiz:

1. a. malignant memory impairment;
   b. intellectual impairment;
   c. poor judgment;
   d. disorientation;
   e. shallow or labile affect.

2. The inability to do simple calculations and to recall simple bits of general information.

3. a. poor attention;
   b. anger;
   c. feeling depressed, lonely, bored, or rejected;
   d. poor concentration;
   e. hypochondriasis;
   f. preoccupation with somatic symptoms;
   g. fear of death.

4. Acute brain syndrome can be reversed with prompt medical intervention.

5. a. malnutrition;
   b. infections;
   c. improper medication;
   d. metabolic disorders;
   e. tumors.

6.

READING 8

Answers to the Quiz:

1. Yes

2. Yes

3.

4. a. It takes most older men longer to get an erection.
   b. Many older men need more tactile stimulation in order to have an erection.

5. The lining of a woman's vagina may become drier and more delicate after menopause. An older woman does not have to give up sex or live with the pain. This problem can be treated with additional lubrication and proper medication.

6. We believe that if you are honest about your feelings in these areas, you will know what kinds of sexual problems you can counsel with understanding and acceptance. If these questions make you uncomfortable, you will be uncomfortable counseling people with sexual problems, and your clients will probably feel uneasy, too. Therefore, if you feel uncomfortable, we recommend that you refer a case requiring sexual counseling to another counselor. There is no reason why you need to change your attitudes about sex. However, if you would like to feel more comfortable or if you plan to do counseling in this area, we recommend that you work on these issues with your supervisor or a psychotherapist.

READING 9

Answers to the Quiz:

1. Personality types are categories which are used to identify a particular set of behaviors typically exhibited by some people.

2. Yes

3. Heredity, environment (learning), self

4. Personality is the characteristic way in which an individual responds to the events of adult life.

5. a. Ways we see ourselves, others, events
   b. Moods
   c. Motivations
   d. Thoughts
   e. Interpretations
   f. Feelings

READING 10

Answers to the Quiz:

1. Do you expect continuity in your personality between now and ten years from now?

2. This question was designed to increase your appreciation of divergent life styles.

3. Having a confidant. Widows who had confidants were found to be happier than married women who did not have confidants.

4. Men become more accepting of their needs for nurturance and dependence while women become more tolerant of aggressive impulses.

READING 11

Answers to the Quiz:

1. You have just completed a partial life review.

2. a. growth
   b. culmination
   c. decline
   d. biological

3. Self-actualization

4. a. intimacy vs isolation
   b. generativity vs stagnation
   c. integrity vs despair

READING 12

Answers to the Quiz:

1. a. Depression
   b. Suicide

2. It is a process of reviewing one's past life through reminiscing, telling stories and talking about the past in order to make sense of one's life.

3. The client may be depressed.

READING 13

Answers to the Quiz:

1. There are different types of issues. Old age is not a second childhood.

2. a. Widowhood;
   b. Retirement;
   c. Empty nest;
   d. Death and dying.

3. a. Denial and disbelief;
   b. Anger (sometimes accompanied by guilt);
   c. Sorrow;
   d. Resolution and acceptance.

READING 14

Answers to the Quiz:

1. a. Consistent physical presence of someone they can trust
    b. Gentle, caring physical contact to assure them of the existence of a gentle and pleasureful world.
    c. Crying and talking, without being interrupted by rationalizations.
    d. Postponement of important decisions.

2. a. Denial and isolation
    b. Anger
    c. Bargaining
    d. Depression
    e. Acceptance
    f. Not all people will go through all stages and not necessarily in the same order.

3. Your deepest, authentic presence. In this area of counseling, genuineness is vital.

4. Grieving before the person's death, i.e. beginning to grieve for someone when we notice they are growing old or ill.

READING 17

Answers to the Quiz:

1. A false belief about oneself.

2. a. Delusions;
    b. Previous hospitalizations for mental problems;
    c. Hallucinations;
    d. Threats of violence;
    e. Suicide threats;
    f. Immobilizing depression.

3. Keep this for future reference.

146

READING 20

Answers to the Final Test:

1. true

2. false . . . if we can generalize from humans to dogs.

3. false . . . senility is a disease. It is not a part of normal aging.

4. false . . . Brain syndrome can be accurately diagnosed through assessment techniques.

5. true

6. true

7. false . . . it depends on the circumstances.

8. true

9. true . . . the lining of the vagina may become drier and more delicate. This can be treated by using additional lubrication and appropriate medication.

10. true

11. true

12. false . . . this is not a diagnostic sign.

13. false . . . an older man needs more tactile stimulation.

14. true

15. true

16. true

17. true

18. true

19. true

20. true

21. false . . . maintenance of IQ from 20-60. Small decline starts somewhere between 60 and 80.

22. false . . . CBS can be mild, moderate or severe.

23. true

24. false . . . life review is a common activity in older individuals.

25. false . . . they can learn, but the learning may take longer.

26. false

27. true

28. false . . . suicide threats are a good indication that someone is seriously considering committing suicide.

29. true

30. false

31. true

32. false . . . there is biologically a lower resistance to stress in older people.

33. false . . . not yet.

34. true

35. true

36. 1) direct instruction; 2) orientation aids; 3) daily reminders.

27. 1) disease; 2) psychological problems (NOT NORMAL AGING)

38. reversible

39. brain syndrome

40. irreversible

41. 1) heredity; 2) environment; 3) self.

42. 1) high illumination without glare; 2) short periods of exposure; 3) enlarge figures; 4) great contrast between figure and background; 5) check on glasses.

43. interfere with memory and cause depression.

44. integrity versus despair.

45. 1) shock, denial and disbelief; 2) anger; 3) sorrow; 4) resolution and acceptance.

REVIEW EXERCISES

Title: Review of Listening Skills (Listening Again)

Rationale: Spaced learning is better than massed trial learning

Objectives:

1. To review the difference between feeling and content.

2. To practice active listening and develop accurate empathy.

Time Requirement: 45 minutes

Procedure:

1. Trainees write out their own responses to the exercise.

2. Trainees discuss their response with each other outside of class.

LISTENING EXERCISE

1. I don't want to go to the senior citizen's center. I went to a dance there a couple of weeks ago, and they reminded me of wilted flowers. It's depressing.

   Content:

   Feeling:

   Possible interpretations:

2. Oh, you'll be gone for a week . . . when will you be back; I'm not sure what I'll do while you are gone. I'm so used to talking everything over with you.

   Content:

   Feeling:

   Possible Interpretations:

3. My daughter's horrible, just horrible! She hasn't seen me for three years. Well, she did come to that anniversary party, but she talked to everyone but me. You'd think she'd want to be with her mother. What do you think about a daughter that would do that to her own mother?

   Content:

   Feeling:

   Possible Interpretations:

4. I just can't get myself motivated. I know I need to go out and check on my apartments, but I can only get myself to do it once or twice a week. I'm bored. Ever since I retired from being a pilot, I haven't felt like doing much and I'm starting to drink too much. I just have to start being practical with my life. I've had enough fun; now I should just work on that property.

   Content:

   Feeling:

   Possible Interpretations:

5. (Phone call). I just can't make it here alone. It hurts so much. My family doesn't want to see me. It's killing me! I'm not going to make it through the night . . . I can't stop crying (sobbing).

Content:

Feeling:

Possible Interpretations:

6. I've been having nightmares ever since my mother went into a home. I know she had to go; the doctor said she had chronic brain syndrome, and she doesn't recognize anyone but me anymore. But the nightmares are awful. And I feel miserable after I go to see her. She never wants me to leave.

Content:

Feeling:

Possible Interpretations:

7. Ever since I retired, my wife and I have had trouble getting along. She acts like the house belongs to her and keeps nagging me about my desk in the living room. It's my favorite place to work, and there's lots of room to spread everything out. I think she just doesn't want me around.

Content:

Feelings:

Possible Interpretations:

8. My daughter came to stay with me when I got out of the hospital two years ago. Everything was fine until she sprained her back and couldn't work. Now she yells at me all the time and uses terrible language. Every time I ask her not to spend any more money — we're living on my social security — she starts yelling at me about what a horrible mother I am. She says I can't move out because that will remind her of when I moved away to get a divorce from her father. You must think I'm awful for saying such things about my own daughter.

Content:

Feelings:

Possible Interpretations:

Title: Reviewing the Levels of Response

Objectives:

1. To review the three possible levels of responding.

2. To reinforce level three responses.

Time required:

45 minutes

Procedure:

Trainees read over the description of the Levels of Response in Chapter 4.
Trainees write in their answers to the exercise.
Trainees discuss their responses.

LEVELS OF RESPONSE EXERCISE

Part I
Label the level of each response given.

1. There's nothing to do and no one to talk to. I just sit in the house by myself all day.

> You sound lonely.

> Well, you're not going to feel any better until you get out of the house!

> It sounds like you are lonely because you cannot find anything that interests you and you do not have any friends you can talk to.

2. I don't know whether to put my mother in a home or not. It's really been hard on my family having her living with us. My wife and I both work, and it's hard on my wife to have to dress and feed my mother everyday. But I'm afraid Mother would be lonely in a home.

> How can you even think of putting your mother away?

> It's hard for you to make this decision.

> It sounds like you're conflicted about where you would like your mother to live. It's hard on your family to take care of her in your home, but you're afraid and maybe feeling responsible that your mother would be lonely living someplace else.

3. We'd always planned to travel when I retired, but now my wife doesn't even want to go out of town for a few days. She's worried that something will happen to her 90-year-old mother while we're away — even though we have a housekeeper for her. We've planned our lives around her mother for so long. Now I wish we could have some time to ourselves.

> You sound disappointed that your wife will not travel with you because it's something you've been planning for a long time. How do you feel about the sacrifices you and your wife have made for her mother?

> Are you disappointed?

> Why don't you just go by yourself?

Part II
Write an example of each of the levels of response.

1. You just don't understand me. That's why you can't help me. Nobody can.

   Level One:

   Level Two:

   Level Three:

2. I don't want to go into the hospital for tests. I've already had one lung removed. I'm sure it's cancer again. I'd rather just forget about it.

   Level One:

   Level Two:

   Level Three:

Part III
Write a Level Three response.

1. I'm not sure I want to talk about it . . . I feel like it's a family matter. But I just can't figure it out by myself. Well, maybe I shouldn't be bothering you with my problems.

2. I don't like to drive anymore. It's hard for me to concentrate, and my hands start shaking when I get in the car. What can I do about it? I would feel so cut off from everyone if I couldn't drive.

3. My husband and I did everything together. I guess he was always my closest friend. I've been trying to get over it. But I think my mind is going. Sometimes I have trouble remembering my guests' names. And I'm so tired because I keep waking up in the middle of the night.

Title: Types of Responses

Objective:

1. To review the types of responses

2. To practice when to use them

Time requirements:

45 minutes

Procedure:

1. Trainees read over the description of the types of responses in Chapter 4.

2. Trainees write a script, using their practicum experience, which describes the appropriate use of the different types of responses.

3. In groups of 6-8 trainees, the trainees who would like to are asked to read examples from their scripts.

EXERCISE FOR TYPES OF RESPONSES

Write a script which illustrates the appropriate use of the different types of responses. Use a problem presented to you in the practicum experience or a problem from your own life. Try to make it brief. Spend about 30 minutes on this part of the exercise.

CASE STUDIES

DEPRESSION: A CASE STUDY

Isobelle Banet, a bright, attractive 62 year-old woman, complained during her first session that she was depressed. She felt as if she "had come to the end of her rope." She said she wished "it would all end." "I wake up in the morning and would like to pull the covers over my head and stay there all day, but I can't." Her sleep pattern was irregular. She would sleep only a few hours a night. She had begun to cry at small provocations, or as she put it, at "nothing at all." Isobelle appeared extremely anxious during the session. She admitted feelings of anger, hostility, and even rage but resisted exploring these feelings more deeply. She seemed to have an agenda of complaining about her mother. She saw her mother as being responsible for Isobelle's condition. She resisted any effort of the counselor to examine her own dynamics.

Helen, Isobelle's 88 year old mother, was quite ill. She had a combination of several illnesses and a serious heart condition. Helen had been a semi-invalid during the past twenty years that Isobelle has been living with her. Isobelle had worked as a medical technician and had supported both of them. She was retired and worked only two days a week. The rest of the week she cared for her mother at home. Much of the care consisted of taking her mother to various doctors during the week. Isobelle complained about her mother's crankiness, her preoccupation with her illness, but mainly her lack of love for her and appreciation for what she did for her.

They would entertain visiting relatives twice a year. Isobelle, who clearly felt her sisters disliked her, described herself as her mother's "live-in maid" during these visits. She claimed that whatever love or tenderness her mother had went to her sisters. Most of Helen's caring and mothering was given to her 70 year old daughter who would stay with them for a month of each year. Isobelle had recently discovered that Helen's life insurance policy named her sister as the sole beneficiary. This upset Isobelle very much. She decided after this discovery that she "couldn't go on this way anymore" and decided to see a counselor. She was insistent that her mother not know she was coming for counseling. "She would throw it up to me forever," she said.

QUESTIONS FOR STUDY:

1. What issues are involved in depression?

2. What particular issues are seen in this case?

3. Describe the method you would use in handling this case.

DEPRESSION: A SUGGESTED TREATMENT APPROACH

1. Empathy — Because the depressed person is experiencing a sense of hopelessness, isolation, low self-esteem and often despair, the counselor should be very aware and tend to these feelings. By responding empathically to what the counselee is feeling, the counselor establishes a rapport based upon his appreciation of these feelings. Much time should be spent validating these feelings.

2. Dealing with hopelessness — The counselor should realize that the depressed client feels very consumed by his depression and has a sense that it will never pass. This is a function of depression. The Counselor, realizing this, explains that these feelings always accompany depression. They are in essence, a function of depression. When the depression passes, as it probably will, the feelings will either pass, or will decrease greatly.

3. Guilt: The depressed person usually has withdrawn considerably from his friends and family. His work has usually suffered from lack of efficiency. Therefore he feels guilty in terms of both his personal relationships and his felt irresponsibility. Very often those around him are critical of him because of how he behaves when he is depressed. The counselor should be empathic with the client's difficulty in fulfilling his responsibilities. He should help the client to understand that such behavior is a function of his depression. Once he is no longer depressed he can live a fairly normal life. The counselee will then be able to re-evaluate his enormous feelings of guilt resulting from his recent depressive behavior.

4. Anger: The client's depression always contains some anger and that anger is usually connected with whatever event or series of events led to a state of depression. The counselor should spend time determining what led to the depression. If it was a serious loss that initiated the depression (death of someone, job loss, a series of crises, or an unbearable living situation), then the counselor should work hard to have the client get in touch with the pain involved in one or more of these events. This part of therapy usually takes some time and the client may be unwilling to get into painful areas. One theory of depression claims that depression serves as a way for a person to avoid dealing directly with the pain and anger associated with his situation. When the anger and pain is not tended to, the depression increases. The counselor should attempt to aid the client in releasing these feelings. Note: One cannot feel anger and depression at the same moment. Anger may also motivate the client to move out of his lethargy and make some changes appropriate to dealing with his troublesome situation.

5. Process and Project: The counselor notes the client's process and infers his possible project. The counselor does this by observing the client's behavior, by listening to how the client has handled his situations in the past, and by being very aware of his own reaction to the client. (The manner in which the client deals with the counselor is the way in which the client deals with others). The counselor then points out to the client his observations concerning the client's process. He discusses these

observations with the client. The counselor and client work together toward a deeper understanding of the connection between the client's processes and his resultant depression. Often elements of passivity, repressed anger, or dissatisfaction of the client with his style of life will emerge as contributors to his depression. If the client chooses to modify some of his processes then he can move from a state of depression into a more active and productive resolution of the problem which activated his depression.

6. Medication: If the client is so severely depressed that the counselor can not work with him effectively, then anti-depressive medication may be helpful. In working with the older adult medication of this kind may be detrimental to his health. The counselor should have a conference with the client's doctor and discuss the advisability of medication. Medication should NEVER be suggested without this connection with the person who is knowledgeable about the client's state of health.

COMMON CAUSES OF DEPRESSION IN OLDER ADULTS

1. Sudden losses: spouse, physical functioning, retirement
   a. ISSUES: anger, mourning, readjustment, helplessness
   b. TREATMENT: work out mourning, anger and frustration issues involved in loss. Tend to process.

2. Unhappy living situations: examples: living with ill spouse, living with Chronic Brain Syndrome, living in an unhappy marriage, living in a home or with a family which is not satisfactory.
   a. ISSUES; anger, frustration, hopelessness, helplessness, feelings of being trapped.
   b. TREATMENT: deal with above feelings, study and deal with process, examine reasons for remaining in situation, examine alternatives.

3. Will to Die: slow deterioration of life sustaining activity.
   a. ISSUES: goals no longer meaningful, positive reinforcements not rewarding, unwillingness to commit suicide directly, not wanting treatment.
   b. TREATMENT: aid in mourning process, medication, much empathy, consideration of process, much support for the person's feelings and at the same time reinforcement for life-oriented behaviors.

ISOBELLE BANET: A CASE FOLLOW UP

INITIAL SESSION:

Counselor noted symptoms of depression. Sleeplessness, anxiety, somatic complaints, excessive crying (not, however, when with counselor), sense of hopelessness and helplessness, denial of feelings, sleep disturbance, altered eating habits, indecisiveness and a pale, drawn, tired appearance.

Counselor noted certain aspects of Isobelle's process: tendency to want to complain about her hurt rather than experience it, resistance to examining her own dynamics, preferring to blame her depression on her mother. Counselor noted Isobelle's history of taking all control and responsibility for financial and practical issues which arose in her family. Counselor noted that Isobelle believed that her worth consisted in giving to others and without this inordinate giving, she would not be loved and would not be a valuable person in her own eyes.

The first session ended with the counselor focusing strongly on Isobelle's feelings of hopelessness, anger and despair.

FOLLOWING SESSIONS:

Although the client has spent two years in counseling, most of the crucial work was accomplished in about six months. The rest of the time in counseling was used for the purpose of supporting Isobelle in her still difficult position.

ISSUES RESOLVED:

1. Isobelle's abandonment of her project to be a martyr. Isobelle is beginning to demand things for herself. She allows others to come in twice a week to care for her mother, and she plans recreational outings for herself. She also is planning for a new career once her mother dies.

2. Isobelle gave up the fantasy that her mother will love her in the "way that she wants her to." She gives in to only those demands of which she feels are fair and appropriate.

3. Isobelle joined an Assertion Training course and has changed much of her passive behaviors.

Isobelle is at present working out issues of grief and mourning which she is aware will come soon when her mother dies. It is not uncommon that relatives of dying individuals go through grief and mourning BEFORE the actual death.

REACTIVE DEPRESSION: A CASE STUDY

Sam, a man of small physical stature, actively involved in social activities and an avid athlete, describes himself as one who "has not accepted the slowing-down process of his age." Presenting problem was that soon after major eye surgery, being totally disabled for two months and dependent on his sister for care, he developed symptoms of extreme depression and anxiety. Along with that, he felt confused and ambivalent about his recent divorce. The recurring thoughts of who would want him when he got older and what would happen to him if he became ill again plagued him.

Sam claims he had been a hard-working, strong, self-sufficient man all his life, and had been perfectly well until his eye surgery forced him into a position of complete helplessness. He found his dependent state so intolerable that the realization he was vulnerable was "earth-shattering." He had always felt immune to everything."

Sam believes that the doctor did not psychologically prepare him for the surgery. He still has days when he has "pressure, pain and clouding," which the doctor has not adequately explained, and these symptoms worry and depress him. He shows concern with the doctor's acumen and would like to shop elsewhere for a second opinion.

The healing process is taking longer than anticipated, and he fears other things might be wrong with him. His deepest fear is that he may go blind.

He says that he is "aware" he has a "negative complex" about illness. No matter what happens, he thinks it "won't clear up." Reflecting back to his childhood, he recalled that when he was about age 6, he woke up "choking, and almost died." The details of the incident were not clearly recalled, but he remembered that he was terribly frightened. All of his life, the fear of illness, if it was of a serious nature, persisted, and he would like some help to overcome the disturbing thoughts.

Sam divorced his third wife a year ago, after a seven-year marriage with many separations and reconciliations. He had no "disagreements with her," their differences were too great. Sam describes himself as being an outgoing, gregarious person, who likes parties, dancing, bridge, tennis and golf. His wife's interests were "just the opposite," and while she had many good qualities, that was not enough for him, and he was bored.

Define the problem:

Define the issues:

What information about aging might you share with Sam?

ANXIETY: A CASE STUDY

Angela Martini, a pretty 70 year old woman, came to counseling at the suggestion of her youngest daughter. Mrs. Martini complained of being anxious and having "restless legs" at night which kept her awake. Mrs. Martini has been married for fifty years and has four grown children. She said one son had drowned at the age of 13. Two of her daughters and one teenage grandchild are living with her and her husband at present. Mrs. Martini cooks and cleans house for the whole family. She said she used to love to make home-made pasta, but now she hates cooking.

Mrs. Martini said she and her husband get along all right now except for his temper and how dependent he is on her. Recently he retired, and he is home all day. Mr. Martini does not let Mrs. Martini leave the house when he is there, and he wants her to go with him whenever he leaves. Mrs. Martini complained that he keeps "bothering her" every night when they go to bed and that he won't stop until she gives in. She said she would prefer to make love only two or three times a week, but she is afraid to tell her husband.

What questions would you like to ask Mrs. Martini?

Define the problem:

What are the issues involved?

What do you think is causing Mrs. Martini's restless legs?

Describe the method you would use in handling this case:

RELATIONSHIP PROBLEMS: A CASE STUDY

Merrilee came to counseling because she was having difficulties with her boyfriend. Merrilee is a charming, cultured 66 year old woman. Most of her life she made a living as an actress on the stage, and she continues to be interested in dramatics and literature. Merrilee said she never wanted to marry; however, throughout her life she has had a series of long term intimate relationships with men she lived with. Merrilee has warm memories of these relationships and talked about the things she had in common with these men and how gently and kindly they treated her.

Merrilee's current boyfriend does not live with her. He has told her he will see her when he is not busy with his son's family. When Merrilee does see him, he comes late and treats her rudely. She said he gets bored at plays and wants to come home early. Merrilee said she is not sure she likes her current boyfriend that much, but she is afraid to end the relationship: "At my age, where could I meet another eligible man? I'm really too old now for anyone to be interested in me. Someone is better than no one. I just have to try not to offend him too much or he might leave me."

Merrilee said she had come to a counselor to find out how she could change her boyfriend and get him to treat her better. She spent most of the first counseling session talking about him, and she only commented on herself when asked direct questions.

Whom should the counseling session be focused on, Merrilee or her boyfriend?

What myths and what realities about aging could be influencing Merrilee?

Define the problem and the issues involved:

What goal might you set with Merrilee?

What are Merrilee's alternatives?

Describe the method you would use in handling this case:

162

RETIREMENT: A CASE STUDY

Terry Waters was a fighter pilot in World War Two. Then, he became a professional pilot for the airlines and liked to fly freight runs where he could experiment with different flying techniques without endangering passengers. He had led an exciting, daring, life. He decided to retire at 62 while he still passed his physical because he did not want to be forced to retire later.

Upon retirement, he believed that age sixty-two he should become responsible and live a controlled, practical life. He said that he was trying to schedule his life accordingly and spend time looking after his investments.

He complained of being bored and said he had begun drinking heavily. He told the counselor that he had come to counseling because he was concerned about his drinking.

Define the problem:

What are the issues involved?

What questions would you like to ask Terry?

What might be some of his alternatives?

WHEN TO GET HELP: A CASE STUDY

When Nancy Sue, age 68, came to counseling, she appeared severely depressed. She had moved west from Alabama because her doctor had recommended it for her asthma and because she wanted to be with her son who lives in Phoenix. She cried when she told the counselor that her son refused to see her when she arrived and that she didn't know why. "We were always so close when he was growing up. He was a sickly child and couldn't go out and play with other boys, so he spent most of his time with me." He left home at 17 and several years later told Nancy Sue he was a homosexual. She said she was ashamed of this.

Nancy Sue's marriage was an unhappy one, and her husband used to beat her. She said she couldn't divorce him because her parents were involved in local politics and a divorce would have caused a scandal. When her husband died, he willed all their property to their two sons and left her dependent on them for support.

Nancy Sue spent the next two sessions talking about how lonely and rejected she felt because she didn't know anyone in Phoenix. She tried to reach her son repeatedly where he worked but he refused to talk to her. She said the man her son was living with came occasionally to see her and took her to the doctor once when she was ill.

Later, Nancy Sue began to tell the counselor that her son followed her everywhere. When she rode the bus, he would sit in the back and ignore her. When she went to a restaurant, he would always be there having a good time with friends and ignoring her. Nancy Sue said she wanted to change apartments because her apartment was bugged. She claimed her neighbors were lesbians who kept trying to "get at" her and who knocked on the walls to keep her awake.

Nancy Sue had no previous history of psychiatric difficulties.

What indications are there that you would want to get help with this case?

What professionals might you consult?

How would you define the problem?

164

Appendix B

TRAINER'S NOTES

TRAINER'S NOTES

These notes are to aid you in using the materials provided in this manual and in integrating the training into mental health programs. Since this manual can be used either for training volunteers or as a university or college course, some of the notes will be more applicable to your particular objectives than others.

GENERAL INTRODUCTION TO THE PROGRAM

NUMBER AND LENGTH OF SESSIONS

The best-tested model for this training program used ten sessions. Each session was three hours long, and included a twenty minute break. One chapter was covered during each session. This model fits well with graduate schedules based on the quarter system. When used for a semester course, the remaining class meetings can be used for further role-playing of counseling sessions and to review case histories in detail.

Two alternative models have been utilized to train paraprofessionals at community sites. They involve either four all-day meetings or two week-end training sessions. It is important not to have more than a week elapse between each training session with these models. Although we expected these models to be too fatiguing for older volunteers since they were scheduled from 9:30 am to 4:30 pm, this was not so. Frequent breaks were offered plus a continual supply of coffee. Volunteers brought bag lunches and extra pillows to make the sessions more comfortable.

WHERE TO HOLD CLASSES

When training volunteers from the community, it is best to find a central location for training. The training room needs to afford privacy and to be large enough for the trainees to break up into smaller groups. Comfortable seating and moveable chairs are essential. University and college settings can possibly offer the advantage of observation rooms with two-way mirrors and sound systems; this is the optimal setting for the practicum sessions. Also, try to find a room with a blackboard or else use large pads of newsprint with marker pens.

RECRUITMENT

Recruitment is an important issue for paraprofessional training. Radio and newspaper announcements, speaking to local groups, and working through the staffs at senior centers and community mental health centers are a combined method of recruitment. When working through center staff, they must be well-informed about the program and the training, or else they will not be able to select appropriate volunteers. It is vital to inform prospective volunteers of the time and emotional commitment involved in counselor training and subsequent service provisions.

An essential part of recruitment is an orientation meeting with prospective volunteers. At that meeting, they are introduced to the trainers and jointly choose a training schedule. The prospective counselors are advised of the following:

1. The training schedule as regards its length

2. An outline of the program itself

3. Personal difficulties which may be encountered during the training course

4. Personal demands involved in the actual counseling sessions themselves, once training is completed.

5. Personal benefits derived from both the training and counseling experiences.

6. Time and duty commitment expected of the counselor once he has completed the training program

7. Evaluation procedure which will be done at the completion of the training.

They are presented with a written summary of the counseling program they may be participating in and an outline of the training course. The following is an example of a hand-out given to community volunteers at an orientation meeting, which you can modify to suit your program:

PEER COMPANIONSHIP PROGRAM

TRAINING:
Who:
Co-trainers. For the first training group the co-trainers will be Kathleen Larkin, M.S., M.F.C. who is an experienced teacher of paraprofessional counselors and Maria Guillindo, a bilingual counselor. Hopefully, subsequent trainers of new volunteers will be experienced peer companions from Rosemead.

CURRICULA:
Purpose:
1. To enhance personal qualities which are essential in good counselors — empathy, respect and genuineness.
2. To increase the counseling skills of active listening and problem-solving.

3. For the counselor's own self-development because increased self-awareness is important for counseling.
4. To familiarize the counselor with facts about aging which are essential for counseling older adults.

Method:

There are fifteen training sessions, each lasting approximately three hours. The class meetings are divided into three parts. The first part involves exercises designed to enhance empathy, respect and genuineness and to increase counseling skills. The second part is to review the homework assignment. The homework is to read a short essay on aging and take a quiz on the material. During the third part, the counselors participate in sensitivity exercises which enhance self-awareness and practice the skills presented earlier. In order to alleviate some of the stress inherent in sensitivity groups, this part of the program will begin with less threatening material which the counselors work on in dyads and progress to exercises involving the whole class.

Topics covered in part one:
1. Listening to your client.
   a.   Listening for feelings.
   b.   Listening for content.
   c.   Nonverbal cues.
   d.   Understanding your client's world view.
2. Responding to your client.
   a.   Summarizing content.
   b.   Reflecting feelings.
   c.   Levels of responding.
3. Problem-solving.
   a.   Identifying issues.
   b.   Exploring alternatives.

Topics covered in facts on aging:
1. Slowing of behavior with age.
2. Sensation — perception
3. Learning
4. Intelligence
5. Memory
6. Organic brain syndrome
7. Diagnosis of brain syndrome
8. Sex and the older adult.
9. Placing the older adult in a home.
10. Personality and clerical information.
11. When to refer a case to a mental health professional.
12. Information and referral services.
13. Review of information.

When:

The first training will be done in four days. The dates are:

Saturday, January 15	9:00 a.m. – 6:00 p.m.
Sunday, January 16	9:00 a.m. – 6:00 p.m.
Saturday, January 22	9:00 a.m. – 6:00 p.m.
Sunday, January 23	9:00 a.m. – 6:00 p.m.

Subsequent training will be scheduled when the program expands and needs additional peer companions.

Supervision:

Peer companions will meet once a week to discuss their caseload. They will meet with Patricia Alpaugh, Ph.D. for supervision. Pattie will be available during the week if any peer companions wish to call her to discuss a case.

Goals:

The goals of this program are the following:

1. To serve lonely, isolated mature adults in the community of Rosemead.
2. To enhance life-satisfaction of the volunteers participating in the program.
3. To make this program autonomous.
   a. Peer companions will eventually take over training.
   b. Peer companions will begin to identify potential clients.
   c. Supervision will be done on a contractual basis.

SERVICE PROVISION:

Initially, Marguerite Mullins, M.S.W. will be responsible for the community work necessary to identify isolated and lonely older adults in Rosemead who would welcome and benefit from a peer companion. Clients will be identified and assigned to a companion on the basis of first assigning clients who have the greatest need. If the program expands, we would like to provide services to seniors who walk-in to the Rosemead Community Recreation Center and want to talk to someone.

Each peer companion will be expected to carry a caseload of approximately three clients. Peer companions may expand their caseloads to whatever size they choose.

The city of Rosemead is our service target area. We plan to provide service to Spanish-speaking and also English-speaking seniors.

Money and Supplies:

Ingleside Mental Health Center will provide the training materials, the trainers, and supervisors through a grant from the City of Rosemead. Ingleside will also reimburse the peer companions 15¢ a mile for their travel expenses to make home visits. The Rosemead Community Recreation Center will provide phones, stationary, and meeting rooms for training and supervision.

JOB DESCRIPTIONS

1. Project initiator and coordinator, Patricia Alpaugh, Ph.D. is a Psychology Intern at Ingleside Mental Health Center, Director of Peer Counselor Training at the Andrus Gerontology Center, and a Marriage and Family Counselor. Her education was in developmental-aging psychology (gerontology) at the University of Southern

California. Her primary role in this program is to initiate and coordinate it. She has designed the training materials. She will develop the initial policies of the program, coordinate the efforts of other members of the program, and monitor fiscal resources. Additionally, she will act as supervisor and consultant for the trained peer companions.

2. Community Outreach Organizer, Marguerite Mullins, M.S.W., is a retired social worker with expertise in community organizing and planning. She will develop a method of identifying isolated, lonely and depressed older individuals in the City of Rosemead. She will play a major role, coordinating with Pattie, in developing the caseloads of the peer companions. Marguerite will also train a peer companion to take over her position as Community Outreach Organizer.

3. Peer Companion Trainers; Kathleen Larkin, M.F.C. and Maria Guillando. Kathleen is a Marriage and Family Counselor and is experienced in developing community mental health centers and training paraprofessional counselors. Her training is in counselor education, and she is currently a counselor, supervisor, and trainer at the U.S.C. Student Health Center. Maria is a counselor there, too, and at El Centro which is a bilingual counseling center in East Los Angeles, and she is a graduate student in counseling. Kathleen and Maria will be the co-trainers of the first group of peer companions. Also, Maria will be translating the training manual into Spanish.

Peer Companions:

All peer companions will attend the training sessions. Then they will service isolated and lonely older adults in the City of Rosemead. They will work through a caseload model and will have three (or more if they choose) persons to visit each week. The bilingual peer companions will visit those mature adults who speak only Spanish.

At the orientation meeting, volunteers are asked to read and sign the following contract:

I agree to attend the training meetings which involve_____
_____(write in schedule).

I agree to participate in the sensitivity group which will involve expressing my feelings, getting feedback on how my behavior affects others, giving feedback on how the behavior of others affects me, examination of myself in the role of counselor.

I agree to let the trainers evaluate me during and after the program to assess whether my talents are more appropriate for counseling, telephone work, information and referral, outreach, or another important role in the counseling program.

I understand that I cannot be a peer counselor unless I complete this training or unless I am already a licensed therapist.

I understand that the trainers and supervisors have the final say as to whether or not I see clients as a counselor.

I understand that I will need the approval of the trainers or supervisor before seeing a new client.

I understand that this training qualifies me to be a peer counselor only at the center I am being trained for.

I agree to attempt to settle any difficulties I may encounter in the training program, or subsequent counseling, with the trainers or supervisor.

I will follow the procedures of the center where I will work, which will include scheduling and carefully maintaining records.

I agree to go through the screening procedures. The following will be included in these procedures: 1) an interview with the trainers and 2) possibly a personality test. The results of these procedures will be confidential.

I understand that I can stop participating in the training and the program at any time.

SCREENING

When possible, screening before training begins is quite helpful. The rationale for using initial screening procedures are (a) to protect the prospective counselor-trainee by detecting personality variables within the applicant which are believed to be at variance with the applicant's probability of succeeding in the course; (b) to protect the interests of the clientele of the center by screening out persons whose personality traits may hinder the progress of the client; (c) to contribute to the efficacy of the training program which assumes certain personality traits to be either beneficial for or detrimental to good counseling.

Generally, a half-hour interview with the applicant is a viable screening technique. Screening devices which are currently being tested include the Rokeach Dogmatism Scale, the Minnesota Multiphasic Personality Inventory, and the Rorschach.

Screening during the training is a delicate process. The authors have found that individual conferences with all trainees, concerning their progress, contribute more to the training program than screening out trainees while the course is in progress. After individual conferences, some trainees who are having difficulty choose to leave the program during the training period. The time for a second official screening comes at the end of training. The contractual agreement at the orientation meeting has forewarned the trainees that completion of the training program does not necessarily mean they will be doing counseling. We try to emphasize the importance of non-counseling roles in mental health service throughout the training, so that the counseling role does not acquire special status. When a trainee clearly does not have the personal qualities and skills required for counseling at the end of the program, the trainers explain these difficulties to him at a private conference where his skills and talents in other areas are emphasized and he is guided into a role in which his talents can be potentiated.

SELECTION OF TRAINERS

The course is more enjoyable, easier, and more effective when taught by co-trainers who are chosen to complement each other's clinical skills and knowledge of gerontology. Co-trainers can role-play and model counseling skills for the trainees and can provide more individualized feedback to them. To maintain a high level of quality, it is essential to have professional clinicians train students who will actually do counseling; their clinical experience plays a vital role in screening. However, it is not necessary to use clinicians as trainers when this course is used to prepare volunteers for other roles in providing mental health services to older adults.

Experience and personal qualities contribute to a trainer's effectiveness. When selecting trainers, the following criteria can be used as guidelines:

1. Active listening skills

2. Ability to teach, to communicate clearly

3. Personal qualities of warmth, respect, empathy and genuineness. Modeling is an important part of this teaching method.

4. When training counselors, good clinical skills, and understanding of psychodynamics, and, if possible, familiarity with group dynamics.

PLACING COUNSELORS AND TRAINEES IN COMMUNITY SITES

It is important to carefully orient volunteers to their placement sites as to role clarification, placement programs, and working conditions. Role clarification includes their relationship to center staff, other center volunteers, and the counseling supervisor. They need to become familiar with the purpose, structure and programming at the sites. Also, they need to know in advance what kind of status, recognition, and reimbursement will be accorded them. Volunteers need a clear definition of the job to be done, and their work must accomplish something, be interesting, and provide the volunteer with motivation, responsibility, growth, achievement, and recognition. It is helpful to develop contractual agreements between site administrators and counselors as to duties, responsibilities, etc.

The placement of volunteer counselors at community sites can be greatly facilitated by the consultation of a social worker with community organizing skills or a community psychologist. Such a person can promote inter-agency cooperation and integration of volunteers into ongoing programs, develop outreach where needed, and identify community resources which can support counseling programs. Such skills are invaluable at community-based sites. Potentially, they could train students and paraprofessionals to take over some of these roles if there are only financial resources available to use these professionals as consultants.

SUPERVISION

We have found it necessary to have both beginning and paraprofessional counselors attend weekly supervision meetings with licensed professionals in order to insure quality mental health services and to protect the beginning counselors themselves. As often as possible, supervisors should be on site while counseling is going on. In many states, this is required by law. The following licensed clinicians, who had background in gerontology, have been effective supervisors in our program: psychiatric social workers, clinical psychologists, licensed marriage, family, and child counselors, and psychiatrists. By promoting inter-agency cooperation between multi-purpose senior centers and either community mental health centers or universities and colleges, a linkage can be developed between volunteer counselors at senior centers and clinical supervisors at the other sites.

IMPORTANCE OF SCREENING CLIENTS

The high suicide rate in older clientele as well as the high proportion of severely disturbed older individuals who will come to a program labelled as "counseling" or "psychotherapy" makes screening of clients and appropriate assignment to counselors imperative in a program involving paraprofessionals and beginning counselors. We recommend that a licensed clinician do intake interviews on all clients, assign cases, and refer inappropriate cases elsewhere. Another method is to have the counselor do the intake using an intake form like the one which will be presented later in the appendix. Then the counselor and the supervisor review the case, and the supervisor screens and assigns cases on the basis of the information gathered by the counselor.

CONTINUED IN-SERVICE TRAINING

This course teaches only the basic counseling skills. It is important for the counselors' growth and development, as well as to maintain the counselors involvement in the program, to provide continued in-service training. An example of a follow-up training package for counselors includes sessions on: minority issues, office procedures, information and referral, outreach and community organizing, legal issues, nutrition and health, and familiarization with other community agencies. The following are some suggested topics for in-service training:

(1) Ethnicity and aging
(2) Development of resources and referral sources
(3) Outreach
(4) Psychopathology
(5) Medication and the elderly
(6) Marital and relationship counseling
(7) Multi-generational family counseling
(8) Grief work
(9) Pre-retirement counseling
(10) Sex therapy
(11) Leading groups
    a. Discussion groups on aging & communication
    b. Orientation of new volunteers
    c. Co-leading psychotherapy groups
    d. Group dynamics
    e. Self-help groups
    f. Advocacy
(12) Specific clinical skills and theory
    a. Behavior modification
    b. Psychodynamics
    c. Assertion training
    d. Logotherapy
    e. Life review and journals as adjuncts to therapy
    f. Transactional analysis
    g. Gestalt techniques
(13) Current research in gerontology

POSSIBLE PROBLEMS

ABSENTEEISM. Since the material presented in each chapter builds on the skills learned in the preceding chapter, it is easy for students to fall behind when they miss chapters. When this happens during the all day weekend training, it is not possible for the average student to catch up. For this reason, it is imperative to emphasize commitment to attend all sessions and complete the course at the orientation session and/or the first day of class. Promoting group cohesiveness from the first day of training is also advisable. Certain group exercises may be useful at that point. We would like to encourage you to draw from your past experience in working with groups to develop and utilize techniques you have found successful in the past and with which you feel comfortable.

Examples of introductory exercises we have used include:

1. Having each student write down four adjectives that best describe them. Then, when they introduce themselves to the group, sharing these adjectives. The trainers model this behavior first, using self-disclosing adjectives. When taught as a college or university course, we have found that it takes a greater degree of self-disclosure than usual on the instructor's part to promote self-disclosure on the part of the students. Another approach is to have the students write these adjectives on a name tag, and then introduce themselves to each other individually. Again, trainers participate in this activity.

2. Introductions in groups no larger than ten, with each person giving their name and an animal they identify with and/or a way to remember their name ("My name is Adele; it rhymes with bell.") and/or why they are interested in counseling. The trainer's model this first.

3. Have the group break up into dyads, and introduce themselves to their partner. Encourage them to share something they feel is unique about themselves. Then their partners will introduce them to the group. Again, we strongly suggest that trainers participate in this model.

As much as possible, respond to each person individually during these exercises, emphasizing their uniqueness as well as their similarity to others in the group. Begin to model active listening through the feedback you give.

Either at the orientation meeting or the first day of class, ask the trainees to write down what they expect to learn in the training and how they expect to apply this learning. When this is a college or university course, a short (2-3 page) paper on how they will apply what they learn now or in the future is an assignment which increases motivation and commitment. As much as possible, try to modify the course materials to fit the needs of the trainees, and by the second session discuss with each student how you think the course will or will not meet their expectations. If the trainee's expectations are too disparate to be integrated with the intent of this course, discuss this individually with the student and encourage a transfer to another course or training program.

GARRULOUSNESS. Frequently, there will be a trainee who monopolizes the class discussions. If this is allowed to continue, it will disturb the other trainees, and they may even drop out of training. When training older volunteers, we have found they would rather leave training than confront another person on their annoying behavior. Therefore, it is important for the trainer to deal with the situation immediately. Be aware of how one group member may annoy the group, or worse, make members of the group feel it is unsafe to open up.

The first strategy we try is to confront the person directly — but empathically — on their need to talk and self-disclose how that behavior is affecting us, using "I" messages. For example: "I think you have a great deal to say; however, when it takes you a long time to make your point, I feel impatient because I want others to have a chance to participate as well." Oftentimes the trainee will agree that they are a bit long-winded. At this point, the group can be enlisted to aid the other person by agreeing on a signal they will give when the person is talking too much. The trainers then model this for the group.

When this is ineffective, we suggest empathically interpreting the individual's behavior either privately or in front of the group if the group is supportive and cohesive. When the talkativeness comes from personal difficulties, we provide private consultation for the individual or strongly recommend individual counseling and provide several referrals. It is vital to firmly limit the garrulous individual's verbal participation during the training sessions. This situation provides an excellent chance to model positive confrontation and interpretation for the test of the group.

RESISTANCE. When trainees do not want to participate in certain exercises, emphasize their right to privacy and right to make their own choices, and interpret their behavior within the framework of their own world view. This not only demonstrates counseling principles presented in this manual but also tends to dissipate the resistance.

EXCESSIVE CRITICISM. It is important to encourage criticism in order to continually improve the training materials and for your professional growth as a trainer and clinician. However, constant criticism or criticism of minute details (pointing out every typo in the manual) on the part of the trainee may be indicative of a personal issue that needs attention. One hypothesis is that this may be a sign of insecurity or lowered self-esteem, possibly the result of the loss of status accompanying retirement. In these cases, we emphasize the value of their role in the program and draw on their experience and expertise to enrich the program. For example, a retired biology professor has given excellent in-service training sessions on sexuality and aging; retired administrators and businessmen have provided valuable consultation on fiscal planning and utilization and coordination of personnel in mental health service centers.

LAG BETWEEN TRAINING AND PLACEMENT. This is not a significant difficulty when these materials are used to teach a university or college course. However, when training volunteers, it is a definite problem. During this lag period, it is important to begin group supervision sessions which can be used as in-service training and orientation to coming placements. Also, we have graduation ceremonies for volunteers, complete with certificates of course completion.

DURING PLACEMENT. Group cohesiveness can deteriorate when volunteers are placed at different sites and/or work different hours. Holding weekly group supervision meetings helps alleviate this problem, and counselors are encouraged to share their experiences, positive and negative, at their placements. Positive feedback and support through supervision will reinforce commitment to the program.

To insure that volunteers feel their work is important and meaningful, they should be given recognition for their accomplishments. Providing them with an official job title and contract is useful as is public recognition. Articles published in local newspapers with pictures of the volunteers and description of services they provide can give recognition as well as publicity for the program.

MEETING PROGRAM OBJECTIVES. Be prepared to reconcile your ideals with what is practically possible given your resources. We started out considering the population we wanted to serve, the population currently being served, and the goals of the personnel involved. We later found it even more relevant to consider: What are the attitudes of the personnel? What are their individual personalities? Then, we tried to recognize and develop the special skills of the staff and to promote cooperation, taking both attitudes and personal idiosyncrasies into account. Our current maxim is: "Work with what you've got." This prevents us from getting trapped in our own discouragement over not being able to provide ideal services. However, this does not mean we stop trying to achieve the highest quality possible.

INTRODUCTION TO USING TRAINING MATERIALS

MATERIALS NEEDED

Although the training manual is all the trainer and trainee need to successfully complete the training program, we have found it helpful to use additional material for many of the exercises. For any exercise in which the trainees share personal information, or in which they observe and critique some event, we have used large pieces of newsprint on which to record each trainees remarks. Providing newsprint and large marking pens to the trainees is a handy means for the group to share much information quickly and easily. Most trainees will also want to make notes or keep diaries which serve as reminders of important ideas which they learn during the sessions. For this reason we recommend that the trainees obtain a small notebook to record important experience and ideas.

SUMMARY OF SUGGESTED MATERIALS:

(1) Training manual for each trainee
(2) Marking pens for each trainee
(3) Small notebooks for each trainee
(4) Ample supply of newsprint for entire group

TIME FRAMES FOR CHAPTERS

We have found that the average amount of time it takes to complete each chapter tends to vary depending upon the idiosyncrasies of each group. Therefore, we have attempted to provide enough material for even the fastest group. Some groups will be able to finish all of the chapters and still have time left over. If your group absorbs the material faster than we have estimated, we encourage you to adjust the sessions by developing longer discussions. If the group still moves quickly, then you can take advantage of the extra time by providing more practicum sessions such as the ones outlined in Chapter Ten. At the time you begin practicum exercises, introduce confidentiality. Ask the class not to discuss personal information to non-participants.

If your group tends to move slowly and not complete the chapters in the allotted time, then we suggest one or more of the following alterations: a) increase the training time, b) have the trainees complete only PART of each exercise and finish the other part for homework, c) evaluate the way in which the trainees utilize the training time. Sometimes certain members involve the group in extraneous and often lengthy discussions. You may wish to correct the situation by putting time constraints on such discussions.

Each chapter is designed to last approximately three hours—180 minutes. We have found the following apportionment of time adequate for the complete of each unit.

30 minutes for review and discussion of readings
20 minutes for class intermission
10 minutes for homework preview
10 minutes for homework review

The remainder of the three hours is spent doing the exercises. Each exercise has the approximate time frame listed in the section under Directions.

HOMEWORK EXERCISES

The homework exercises are designed to augment the important notions conveyed in each chapter. For that reason it is important to impress upon trainees the advantage of faithfully completing the homework assignment for each chapter. We have found that a productive method of handling the homework section is to preview each homework lesson at the end of each training period, and to review the completed homework at the beginning of the next training session. The homework should include the exercises at the end of each chapter and the introductory remarks at the beginning of the next chapter. To preview the homework, simply read the directions with the trainees to be sure they understand what is being asked of them. Also point out the introductory remarks in the subsequent chapter. The review of homework will consist of discussing any problems encountered by the trainees and some discussion about the ideas contained in the introduction to the lesson for the day. Because most of the exercises have answers, there is usually not much discussion concerning most exercises. The trainees are also assigned to read and study the Readings for each chapter and do the exercises at the end of the readings. We do NOT include reviewing this part of the homework during this period since a separate section of each training session is set aside especially for that purpose.

SUMMARY OF HOMEWORK INSTRUCTIONS

1. Preview homework:
   a. Assign readings in the next chapter.
   b. Have class read the introduction to the following chapter as homework.
   c. Read over homework exercise instructions to be sure each trainee understands what is required of him.

2. Review homework:
   a. Review homework exercises.
   b. Review introductory section to chapter.

Homework Exercises and Answer Sheets can be removed from the text if the instructor wishes to use them for grading purposes.

INTRODUCTORY PAGE TO EACH CHAPTER

Originally, the introductory page to each chapter was presented as a mini-lecture by the trainers. As an alternative to this mode of presentation, the trainee can be asked to read the introduction before class and discuss it in class. Or, trainees can read it together in class.

READINGS ON AGING

The facts on aging sections are to be read by the trainees before that chapter is covered in class. Generally, a 20 minute discussion period is sufficient. The general issues to be covered in class discussion are:

1. Clarification of the material

2. Elaboration of the concepts

3. How the information would apply to clinical situations

ASKING FOR FEEDBACK

At the end of each session, ask for feedback. Our empirical research has demonstrated that this training package significantly increases empathy, warmth, and active listening skills; however, we have been constantly revising it and using feedback from the groups we have trained. We feel that no counseling training manual can be a finished product and that it can always be improved and refined. Also, it needs to be adapted to the needs of specific training groups.

From the feedback you get, it may become apparent that certain chapters will be more effective if modified somewhat as you progress through the training.

Begin to make your own training notes in the manual for future training sessions.

GROUP DYNAMICS WHICH EVOLVE DURING TRAINING

Because of the nature of the training exercises, the trainer will soon become aware that the group discussion periods are in essence, structured sensitivity sessions. It is our observation that much of the real effectiveness of the program centers around these sessions. It is good practice for the trainer to view these sessions as sensitivity sessions and use his knowledge of group dynamics to maximize the potential of exercises which involve personal communications from the trainees. The trainer who is aware of the collective personality of the group and can determine how each member contributes to that collective, can teach the trainees much about themselves regarding their interactions with other group members. The group will have to evolve as a unit after several readjustments. Those readjustments will occur each time a member reveals a personal communication and others respond to it by giving him feedback. It will evolve after confrontations and resolutions of confrontations. It will evolve finally when each member is aware of who he is "among others" and finds validation and support from the group. A cohesive group is not one which is in full agreement, nor one in which everyone likes everyone else, but rather a group whose honest feelings are apparent and where every member is respected for his individuality.

What we present here is, of course, the ideal. The training period itself may not be long enough to accomplish such demanding group goals, but those goals are worth reaching for, and any attainment of them is beneficial for everyone concerned.

CHAPTER GUIDES

CHAPTER 5

At the time you teach interpretation, it is sometimes helpful to present certain psychological concepts, depending on the sophistication of your class and the time available for additional lecturettes.

Interpretations can be categorized in three ways:

1. BASED ON FEELINGS: Interpretations that are derived from inferences about feelings which underly a client's statement but which are not expressed directly.

2. BASED ON PATTERNS: Interpretations that come from observed patterns in the client's behavior and verbalizations. You may want to introduce some transactional analysis games, as they are easy-to-understand, common patterns of human behavior.

3. BASED ON THEORY: Interpretations based on inferences drawn from observation of behavior and verbalizations viewed within the context of a particular theoretical position. For example, a woman who repeatedly has relationships with married men may be seen as acting out early, unresolved Oedipal conflicts according to Freudian Theory.

Additionally, it can be useful to introduce and define certain defense mechanisms which can aid the trainee in drawing inferences: 1) distinguishing between suppression and repression; 2) denial (implication in psychosomatic complaints and positive aspects when it is used to gain information that a person cannot face immediately but gradually begins to deal with in stages); 3) displacement; 4) projection; 5) sour grapes; 6) rationalization and intellectualization; 7) sublimation; 8) dependency; and 9) identification. We emphasize the trainees using this knowledge to develop inferences and not to use this vocabulary in their interpretations to the client.

SUPERVISION MODEL

It has been the authors' experience that weekly supervision is essential for a program which utilizes the services of paraprofessional, peer, and beginning counselors. Under optimal conditions, counselors are supervised in groups no larger than six, by a professional clinician, for 1½ hours a week.

Research has shown that supervisors are not accurate in their estimation of what their supervisees do in actual client sessions. Therefore, the authors recommend that, monthly, the supervisor observe all or part of a counseling session by each counselor in the supervision group. Videotapes, two-way mirror observation rooms, and tape recorders can be used in this process. When using tapes of sessions, it can be useful to ask the counselor to mark places on the tape illustrating (1) a particularly effective part of the counseling session, (2) a place where the counselor had difficulties, and (3) a section typifying the counseling session.

A model of supervision which is consistent with this training package will be outlined here:

1. Supervisees are asked if they have a case they would like to share with the group or if there is a case about which they have a question.

2. The volunteer(s) then role-play the client in the case while someone else acts as the counselor.

3. The rest of the group and the supervisor observe the role-playing and write their comments on the "Supervision Comments" sheet.

4. Then the group discusses the examples of Level 1, Level 2, and Level 3 responses.

5. The person who played the client then gives feedback to the counselor.

6. The supervisor points out the psychodynamics of the case.

7. The "Supervision Comments" sheets are then given to the person who played the counselor.

8. Throughout, the supervisor emphasizes the positive and constructive aspects of feedback.

SUPERVISION COMMENTS

Level 3.
  (Feelings integrated with content)

Level 2.
  (Feelings)

Level 1.

RATE ON:

	1	2	3	4	5
Empathy	Does not attend to or distracts from feelings		Can verbalize what client is feeling		Express feelings & helps client to understand them
Genuineness	Counselor denies what he feels about client or only shares negative feelings		Counselor gives neither negative nor nor positive cues about what he feels		Counselor expresses her feelings openly
Respect	Communicates lack of respect		Positive respect for client's feelings & concerns		Deepest respect for worth as a person & freedom as an individual

182

INTAKE INTERVIEW FORM

Date of Contact _____ Mode of Contact: ____Phone ____Walk-In

Service Location _____ USC _____Other Site: _____

Name(s) of Client(s) #1_____ Phone _____

  Address_____City_____Zip_____

  Age_____Sex: ___Male ____Female

  #2_____ Phone _____

  Address_____ City_____Zip_____

  Age_____ Sex: ___Male ___ Female

  #3_____ Phone _____

  Address_____ City_____Zip_____

  Age_____ Sex: ___Male ____Female

Name of Caller/Contact Person _____ Phone _____

  Address_____ City_____Zip_____

  Relationship To Client(s):_____

  _____

How did caller learn about this service?_____

Current Need/Problem: (Check as many as apply)

  ____ Employment   ____ Housing   ____ Medical   ____ Transportation
  ____ Financial   ____ Legal   ____ Mental Health ____ Volunteer
  ____ Homemaker/Chore   ____ Leisure   ____ Nutrition   ____ Other

Comments: (Describe Need/Problem)_____

_____

_____

_____

Action Taken: _____

_____

_____

Follow-Up: _____

_____

_____

_____

Person who completed form _____

INTAKE INTERVIEW

1. What's your main problem?

2. Statement of problem:

   a. How long has this been a problem?

   b. Describe the first time you felt this way (or had this problem).

   c. How much does this interfere with your life?

   d. What kind of situations does this affect you in?

   e. How does it affect you and others?

   f. How often?

3. Do you ever feel depressed?

   a. How is your appetite? Is this different from how you usually are?

   b. Have your sleep patterns changed?

   c. Do you feel more or less tired than you used to?

   d. Do you have any (other) recent physical complaints?

4. When you're depressed, what do you feel like doing?

   (If suicide is mentioned, ask how they intend to do it.)

5. Where do your family and friends live?

   a. Who are you living with?

   b. What social services have you contacted?

   c. Who would you call for help in an emergency?

6. Do you have trouble with your memory?

   If yes: I want to ask you a few questions:
   (use Mental Status Question form; write in the answers)

7. How are you getting along with your family/close friends?

EVALUATION OF PEER COUNSELOR TRAINING

Please fill out this evaluation form, and return it to your supervisor or trainer. Please check the appropriate rank; a rank of "1" is the lowest. Do NOT put your name on this form.

How helpful were the training materials?

1	2	3	4	5
not very helpful				extremely helpful

Were the training materials clearly written and easy to understand?

1	2	3	4	5

What do you think are the strengths and weakness of the training materials?

How would you rate your trainers on the following:

Empathy

Trainer's name	1	2	3	4	5

Co-trainer's name	1	2	3	4	5

Respect

Trainer's name	1	2	3	4	5

Co-trainer's name	1	2	3	4	5

Genuineness

Trainer's name	1	2	3	4	5

Co-trainer's name	1	2	3	4	5

Knowledge of Aging

| Trainer's name | 1 | 2 | 3 | 4 | 5 |

| Co-trainer's name | 1 | 2 | 3 | 4 | 5 |

Knowledge of Counseling Skills

| Trainer's name | 1 | 2 | 3 | 4 | 5 |

| Co-trainer's name | 1 | 2 | 3 | 4 | 5 |

Ability to Communicate Clearly

| Trainer's name | 1 | 2 | 3 | 4 | 5 |

| Co-trainer's name | 1 | 2 | 3 | 4 | 5 |

What do you see as their particular strengths?

Trainer's name:

Co-trainer's name:

How do you think they could improve?

Trainer's name:

Co-trainer's name:

Any additional comments:

EVALUATION OF SUPERVISION

Please fill out this evaluation form, and return it to your supervisor. Do NOT put your name on this form.

Please check the appropriate rank; a rank of "1" is the lowest, and a rank of "5" is the highest. Please only rank supervisors you have seen in supervision.

SUPPORTIVE OF YOUR WORK

```
|———————|———————|———————|———————|
1       2       3       4       5
```

KNOWLEDGE OF AGING

```
|———————|———————|———————|———————|
1       2       3       4       5
```

KNOWLEDGE OF COUNSELING SKILLS

```
|———————|———————|———————|———————|
1       2       3       4       5
```

AVAILABILITY FOR ADDITIONAL HELP

```
|———————|———————|———————|———————|
1       2       3       4       5
```

UNDERSTANDS AND RESPONDS TO SPECIAL NEEDS OF THE SUPERVISEES

```
|———————|———————|———————|———————|
1       2       3       4       5
```

EMPATHY

```
|———————|———————|———————|———————|
1       2       3       4       5
```

RESPECT

```
|———————|———————|———————|———————|
1       2       3       4       5
```

GENUINENESS

```
|———————|———————|———————|———————|
1       2       3       4       5
```

CAPABLE OF GIVING NEGATIVE FEEDBACK WHEN NECESSARY

```
|———————|———————|———————|———————|
1       2       3       4       5
```

What do you think your supervisor's strengths are?

What do you think your supervisor needs to work on?

Evaluation Prepared by:_____

(Name of Supervisor)

Title: _____

Date: _____

Name of Student Evaluated: _____

Specific Assignments of Student (include caseload)_____

_____

_____

_____

_____

_____

INSTRUCTIONS: Write in appropriate number for each factor:

(1) Poor;   (2) Below average;   (3) Average;   (4) Above average;   (5) Outstanding.

Please comment on the student's performance wherever possible.

_____

_____

I. PROFESSIONAL PERFORMANCE AND SKILLS
(Note: Each score in this category is rated double points.)

A. Good judgment in making assessment of counseling potential of older clients.

B. Can formulate therapy/counseling goals which are appropriate and relevant to the older client.

C. Can effectively differentiate the special needs and interests of the older client and other family members.

D. Is able to establish and maintain good rapport with older clients.

_____

*Form developed by administrative staff of Adult Counseling Center at the Andrus Gerontology Center, University of Southern California.

E. Handle "information and referral" for older clients and families appropriately.

F. Shows awareness of and sensitivity to environmental factors affecting older adults.

G. Deals with older client's support systems or lack of support systems.

H. Moves toward relatively specific goals in counseling older adults and their families.

I. Is able to confront older clients, yet takes them seriously, treats them with dignity.

II. PROFESSIONAL DEVELOPMENT

A. Can accept and utilize supervisor's suggestions.

B. Willingness to learn and change professionally.

C. Not dependent on supervisor — uses supervisor as consultant.

D. Keeps self aware of new developments in gerontology.

E. Makes attempt to understand and utilize community resources appropriate to older persons.

III. RELIABILITY OF PERFORMANCE

A. Follows rules (reporting, etc.) of the Center.

B. Is on time; keeps appointments.

C. Sensitive to co-workers; maintains good working relationships.

D. Willing to assume responsibility where appropriate; can initiate.

Additional Comments:

A. What are specific strengths of the student:

B. In which specific areas would he/she benefit from additional work or training:

C. Recommendations to student:

IV. Counselor Qualities. Please rate counselor on the following scales, according to the Carkhuff ratings (1 to 5).

_____ respect

_____ empathy

_____ genuineness

_____ self-disclosure

_____ confrontation

_____ immediacy of relationship

_____ counselee self-exploration

_____ personally elevant concreteness or specificity of expression

V. Review with student _____
                              (Date)

A. Reaction to Discussion:

B. Student's Suggestions:

_____   _____
(Signature of Supervisor)   (Signature of Student)

Appendix C

NOTES ON PROVIDING MENTAL HEALTH SERVICES IN THE COMMUNITY

Much has been said about how many older adults are in need of mental health services and how few are actually being served. Part of the problem is that there are so few clinicians trained in gerontology and that many professionals shy away from working with the elderly. However, it is also true that older individuals underutilize some of the traditional mental health services available to them. One important point to remember is that the current cohort of older adults attaches a greater stigma to counseling and psychotherapy than other groups. Even if they overcome this hurdle, their decreased mobility may make it difficult to get to service sites.

As a result, we have found it necessary to diverge from total reliance on traditional modes of providing psychiatric help such as one-to-one counseling and publicizing services as "counseling" or "psychotherapy." In many cases, the counselor cannot wait for the client to come to him; he must seek out the client. This is particularly true in a community where there are a large number of shut-ins. To locate older individuals in need, outreach becomes an essential part of mental health service provision for older adults. The training provided through this manual will develop the sensitivity and many of the skills an outreach worker needs when they visit older adults in their homes. The work of knocking on many doors to find shut-ins can be physically and emotionally taxing; therefore, the persons in your program doing this task will need at least as much supportive supervision as those doing actual one-to-one counseling. When a shut-in is identified, the worker needs to assess the person's needs and strengths to determine what kinds of services the individual needs, can utilize, and will accept. Some of the alternative interventions are as follows:

1. Connecting the individual with concrete services, such as meals-on-wheels or a mobile library.

2. Supporting the individual to become involved in community services and activities, such as participating in multi-purpose senior center programs.

3. Weekly visits by a counselor to begin counseling in the home with individuals who are emotionally distraught but who are unable to come to service sites due to physical or emotional disabilities.

4. Connecting the individual with a phone reassurance program which can be run by counselors. This can range from a brief call each day to see that the individual is physically all right to phone counseling.

5. Helping the shut-in to develop or redevelop a support system with family, friends and/or neighbors, especially helping them to form a relationship with a confidante.

All of these interventions must be done as unobtrusively as possible. This is another place in which the counselor training is useful because it teaches the counselor to respect the life styles of others, including their need for privacy. This emphasizes the role of preventive mental health in providing services to older individuals in the community.

Outreach in the community can also be done through meals-on-wheels and visiting nurses programs. Service-deliverers in these programs can identify, sometimes with the aid of familiarization with mental health principles, individuals who need mental health services. Whenever it is possible to establish a good working relationship with these programs, counselors can accompany these service providers on their visits. In the Los Angeles area, the local government agency responsible for the coordination of services (the Area Agency on Aging) supports outreach escorts, a program involving home visits, phone contacts, and other methods to locate isolated older adults in the community. Other outreach sources include the Department of Public Social Services (DPSS) and local churches and synogogues.

Another non-threatening approach is to provide informal counseling at recreation centers, senior centers, and multipurpose senior centers. This is most effective when the counselors are residents of the communities served by these centers and when they participate in the activities, such as clubs, classes, exercise programs, and nutrition programs. This provides many opportunities for informal counseling. For example, if a participant in the program has been recently widowed, the counselor can comfortably have lunch with that person and listen if they need someone to talk to. Again, it is important what name is given to the "counselors." Names such as "participants," "listeners," or "companions" are usually more acceptable than "counselor" to community members.

Counselors can also reach individuals by giving informational lectures and leading discussion groups. Any of the readings on aging in this manual can be used as the basis for a lecture that may touch on issues personally relevant, and possibly emotionally distressing, to those older adults who come to the lecture. Discussion groups on these topics, as well, can provide an opportunity for individuals to talk about issues which are bothering them.

Some topics which have been fruitful include:

1. How to talk to your doctor

2. What I am proud of in my life

3. Woman's liberation (This can provoke a particularly lively discussion in a group of men and can lead to a fruitful discussion of interpersonal relationships.)

4. How to give and accept compliments

5. Growing old gracefully?????

6. Memory complaints

7. Writing your autobiography

Teaching assertion training skills as a part of these discussions can help the older adult to deal with his environment more effectively and increase his self esteem by decreasing his sense of helplessness. Peter Smith's book, *When I Say "No", I Feel Guilty* is a helpful resource to use.

"Writing Your Autobiography" can be presented as a series of workshops which will aid the older individual in beginning a life review. Writing topics which can be used as part of these workshops include:

1. Turning points in my life

2. My sex and sex-role identification history

3. My love and hate history

4. My health history

5. My experiences with death

6. My crisis history

7. My spiritual development

8. My career history

Most of these topics were developed and used by Dr. Birren and his associates at U.S.C. in a course which promoted psychological development through autobiography. A helpful resource is Ira Progoff's *At a Journal Workshop.*

It is beyond the scope of this training manual to delineate the principles and strategies of community mental health for older adults. We hope to have stimulated your interest in this area, to have pointed out the need for it, and to have shared a few ideas which will stimulate your own creativity in this area.

RESOURCES

Becker, F. M., and Zant, S. H. The use of older volunteers as peer-counselors. A paper presented at the 29th Annual Meeting of the Gerontological Society, 1976.

Birren, J. E. *The psychology of aging.* New Jersey: Prentice-Hall, Inc., 1964.

Birren, J. E., and Schaie, K. W. (Eds.) *Handbook of the psychology of aging.* New York: Van Nostrand Reinhold Company, 1977.

Brammer, L. M. *The helping relationship.* New Jersey: Prentice-Hall, Inc., 1973.

Bullmer, K. *The art of empathy.* New York: Human Sciences Press, 1975.

Busse, E. W., Dovenmuehle, R. H., and Brown, R. G. Psychoneurotic reactions of the aged. *Geriatrics,* 1960, *15,* 97-105.

Butler, R. N., and Lewis, M. I. *Aging and mental health.* St. Louis: The C. V. Mosby Company, 1977.

Carkhuff, R. R. *Helping and human relations (Vols. I & II).* New York: Holt, Rinehart and Winston, 1969.

Carkhuff, R. R. *The Art of Helping.* Amherst: Human Resource Development Press, 1972.

Carkhuff, R. R., and Berenson, B. G. *Beyond Counseling and Therapy.* New York: Holt, Rinehart and Winston, 1967.

Danish, S., and Hauer, A. *Helping skills: A basic training program.* New York: Behavioral Publications, 1973.

Duke, M. P., and Frankel, A. S. *Inside psychotherapy.* Chicago: Markham Publishing Company, 1971.

Eisdorfer, C., and Lawton, M. P. (Eds.) *The psychology of adult development and aging.* Washington, D.C.: American Psychological Association, 1973.

Ettkin, L., and Snyder, L. A model for peer-group counseling based on role-playing. *The School Counselor,* 1972, *19,* 215-218.

Goldfarb, A. I. Managing the disturbed elderly patient in family practice: A simple screening test for chronic brain syndrome: No. 5 in a series.

Goldfarb, A. I. Managing the disturbed elderly patient in family practice: When to consider institutional care: No. 3 in a series.

Goldfarb, A. Psychotherapy of aged persons. *Psychoanalytic Review,* 1955, *35,* 644-653.

Haase, R. F., and Tepper, D. T. Nonverbal components of empathic communications. *Journal of Counseling Psychology,* 1972, 19: 417-424.

Hackney, H. Nye, S. *Counseling Strategies and Objectives.* New Jersey: Prentice-Hall, 1973.

Isaac, S., and Michael, W. *Handbook in research and evaluation.* San Diego, California; Robert R. Knapp, 1971.

Ivey, A. E. Normington, C., Miller, C., Morrill, W., Haase, R. Microcounseling and attending behavior: An approach to practicum counselor training. *Journal of Counseling Psychology* 1968, 15: 1-12.

Kahn, R. L., and Zarit, S. H. Evaluation of mental health programs for the aged. In P. Davidson, F. Clark, and L. Hamerlynck (Eds.), *Evaluation of Behavioral Programs.* Illinois: Research Press, 1974.

Kavanaugh, R. E. *Facing death.* Baltimore: Penguin Books Inc., 1972.

Keleman, S. *Living your dying.* New York: Random House, Inc., 1974

Kimmel, P. C. *Adulthood and Aging: an interdisciplinary developmental view.* New York: John Wiley and Sons, 1974.

Kral, V. A. Managing the disturbed elderly patient in family practice: Memory dysfunction as a diagnostic sign: No. 2 in a series.

Kubler-Ross, E. *Death: The final stage of growth.* New Jersey: Prentice-Hall, Inc., 1975.

Kubler-Ross, E. *On death and dying.* New York: Macmillan Publishing Co., Inc., 1969.

Kubler-Ross, E. *Questions and answers on death and dying.* New York: Macmillan Publishing Co., Inc., 1974.

Larkin, L. Training Manual for Crisis Line, unpublished manuscript, NE Georgia Community Mental Health Center, 1972.

May, R. *The Art of Counseling.* Nashville: Parthenon Press, 1967.

Neugarten, B. I. *Middle age and aging: A reader in social psychology.* Chicago: The University of Chicago Press, 1972.

Progoff, I. *At a journal workshop.* New York: Dialogue House, 1977.

Rogers, C. The necessary and sufficient conditions of therapeutic personality change. *Journal of Consulting Psychology,* 1957, *5,* 22.

Rogers, C., Truax, G., Gendlin, G., and Kiesler, D. *The therapeutic relationship and its impact.* Madison: University of Wisconsin Press, 1967.

Rosenblatt, R. Basic training in communications and counseling skills for peer counselors, unpublished manual of the University Counseling Center at the University of Southern California, 1976.

Samuels, M., and Samuels, D. *The complete handbook of peer counseling.* Miami: Fiesta Publishing Corp., 1975.

Schmidt, L., and Strong, S. Expert and inexpert counselors. *Journal of Counseling Psychology,* 1970, *17,* 115.

Smith, M. *When I say no, I feel guilty.* New York: The Dial Press, 1975.

Vassos, S. T. The utilization of peer influence. *The School Counselor,* 1971, *18(3),* 209.

Wackman D., Miller, S., and Nunnally, E. *Basic communication skills for relationship growth: A classroom program.* Minneapolis: Interpersonal Communication Programs, Inc., 1975.

Whitehead, A. *In the service of old age.* Baltimore: Penguin, 1970.

Zarit, S. H. (Ed.) *Readings in aging and death: Contemporary perspectives* New York: Harper & Row, 1977.

Zunker, V. G., and Brown, W. F. Comparative effectiveness of student and professional counselors. *Personnel and Guidance Journal,* 1966, *44,* 738-743.

FINAL EXAMINATION

for the book

COUNSELING THE OLDER ADULT

CONTAINS:

1) Final Test
2) Blank Answer Sheets for Test
3) Answers for Instructors and Trainers

This final examination section for
COUNSELING THE OLDER ADULT
is published by the
Ethel Percy Andrus Gerontology Center
University of Southern California

RICHARD H. DAVIS, Ph.D.
Director of Publications and Media Projects

Lexington Books
D.C. Heath and Company
Lexington, Massachusetts
Toronto

COUNSELING THE OLDER ADULT

Final Examination

Part I Answer the following questions True or False.

1. Under conditions of normal aging, older adults can learn new information and skills.

2. Retirement for some older people can be a crisis, for others it is a relief.

3. Old age is another childhood.

4. Retirement is one of the few socially — determined developmental tasks of old age in the United States.

5. Intimate, stable relationships which provide good communication serves as a buffer against the losses of aging.

6. In nursing homes, all residents should be forced to participate in all activities because remaining active is always the best adjustment to old age.

7. When the counselor takes the client and his problem seriously, he is showing concern.

8. During the re-establishment phase of grief, new and old friends are very important for the grieving person.

9. The client may communicate through his posture or tone of voice.

10. Feelings always make sense when viewed in context of the individual's world view.

11. Life review is an abnormal activity for older individuals.

12. Life review involves a tendency to reminisce, to tell stories, and to think of past events.

13. It is possible that medical or psychological problems, rather than brain damage can be responsible for intellectual decline and memory problems.

14. Suicide is often preceded by withdrawal, bereavement and induced helplessness.

15. Orgasms are rare for older adults.

16. Current research indicates that some memory complaints are often signs of depression rather than actual memory loss.

17. Boredom with a sexual partner may be a cause of impotence in the older male adult.

18. People who threaten suicide are usually not the ones who commit suicide.

19. Older adults usually function better in situations which do not have excessive time limits.

20. It is preferable to talk away fears about dying with a dying client than to listen to his fears of death.

21. Older adult males generally need less stimulation in order to have an erection.

22. Research shows that it takes longer for most older men to get an erection.

23. Anger is an abnormal and unhealthy reaction for a client who has suffered from the death of another.

24. After a person recovers from the crisis of a heart attack, sexual intercourse usually does not endanger his health.

25. With proper medical treatment. Chronic Brain Syndrome can be reversed.

26. Sexual problems in older adults are to be expected and counselors should encourage older adults who have sexual problems to develop an interest in hobbies and other recreations as a substitute for sexual activity.

27. Intercourse may be painful for women over sixty.

28. Finishing "unfinished business" is an important part of ending a counseling relationship.

29. Once a counseling relationship has ended, the counselor should never call the client.

30. Goal-setting in a counseling relationship is primarily the prerogative of the client.

31. When clients feel relieved because of the death of a close relation, then they probably need the help of a psychiatrist because that reaction is an indication of severe problems.

32. One reason for studying personality is the assumption that there are certain central themes in the organization of an individual's responses, that if known, may enable one to predict many future responses.

33. Generally, personality characteristics change frequently during the life span.

34. A counselor may discuss and exchange information about his client with any person if he believes it will help his client. He does not have to have his client's permission for this.

35. It is helpful for a counselor to make his clients aware that with aging, they will slowly lose their capacity to function and to remember.

36. In a counseling office which serves older adults it is a good idea to provide chairs with arms.

37. The lining in the vagina of an older woman may become delicate after menopause.

38. Older adults have a biologically lower resistance to stress than do younger adults.

39. Visual acuity can be aided by low illumination because low illumination filters out glaring rays.

40. Arteriosclerosis in the eye is a good indication and diagnosis of arteriosclerosis in the brain.

41. Everyone who dies goes through the five stages in order, outlined by Kubler-Ross.

42. The basic determinants of personality that have been studied are heredity, environment and the self.

43. The counselor should cross-examine the client in order to find out what is really going on and then catch the client in his own lies.

44. Silence can be an appropriate counselor response.

Part II Choose the response which you believe is the most accurate. On your answer sheet, indicate your response with a letter; a., b., c., d., e., or f.

45. When a counselor is asked by the family or friends of an older adult to decide whether the client should be placed in a home, the counselor should: a) search for the best home for the client b) be careful to explain to the client that the counselor is acting in the best interest of the client c) be careful to comfort the client should he become distressed about the proposal d) do all of the above things e) not assume the responsibility for such a decision.

46. Which of the following validates the client? a) denying the existance or importance of the client's feelings. b) implying there is something wrong with what the client is feeling c) stating that the client shouldn't worry because things always turn out for the best. d) accurately reflecting the client's feelings.

47. Older adults whose mental capacities are still intact: a) can experience some forgetfulness b) can still suffer from some senility c) cannot learn new material well d) all of the above.

48. Which of the above is the most severe contributor to permanent memory loss? a) depression b) anxiety c) aging d) brain disease e) all of the above are equal contributors to memory loss.

49. Senility is a term which: a) refers to the thinking processes in adults over sixty-five. b) originates from a Latin medical term. c) is another way of referring to older paranoids. d) none of the above.

50. Which of the following is an accurate statement? A major problem which older adults often experience is a) insanity b) return to childhood c) depression.

51. Which of the following is NOT a symptom of Organic Brain Syndrome? a) poor judgment b) disorientation c) shallow or labile affect d) hearing loss e) severe memory disturbance.

52. The part of the life-span in which intelligence is rather stable is: a) early childhood b) adolescence c) young adulthood through middle age d) old age e) there is no research to indicate that intelligence is stable at any age.

3

53. Loss of hearing in older adults is usually a) a side effect of brain damage b) implies brain damage c) makes high tones rather than low tones more audible d) is extremely rare e) none of the above.

54. The usual age at which sensory processes may begin to impair behavior somewhat is approximately a) fifty-five b) sixty c) seventy d) eighty e) ninety.

55. Senility differs from senescence in the sense that a) senility occurs in most older adults, senescence does not b) there is no real difference, senility and senescence mean the same thing c) none of the above.

56. A statement which would accurately describe malignant forgetfulness is: a) it is a more severe form of benign forgetfulness b) happens to the majority of older adults c) is a symptom of brain disease d) none of the above.

57. Which statement about the MSQ is NOT accurate? a) the MSQ consists of ten reality questions plus four additional questions which the counselor may want to use. b) the MSQ is scored according to the number of errors on the first ten questions. c) the MSQ is so precise an instrument that it alone is sufficient to indicate brain damage d) a score of zero to two on the MSQ indicates none or minimal brain damage.

58. Which intellectual task would be more difficult for an older adult? a) using new material in new ways b) using old material in new ways c) using new material in old ways d) all of the above e) none of the above.

59. In laboratory situations which tested learning performance in older adults, older adults scored: a) poorer than other age groups b) better than other age groups c) equal to other age groups.

60. Adaptive strategies in old age can include which of the following? a) disengagement b) life review c) activity d) use of assistants to help accomplish tasks e) all of the above.

Part III Complete the following statements. Write your responses on the accompanying answer sheet.

61. Restating content and feelings adds to the effectiveness of counseling. Give one reason why this is true.

62. A response in which a counselor divulges personal information is called _____ ?

63. A response in which the counselor makes an inference and expresses his inference to the client is called a/an _____ .

64. The type of brain syndrome which can be cured is _____ brain syndrome.

65. A false belief about oneself such as an extreme overestimation of one's importance is called a/an _____ .

66. A client who is apathetic, tired, feels worthless and helpless may be suffering from _____ .

4

67. What is a "theme" in counseling?

68. What is one characteristic of a Level III response?

69. Briefly define the term "world-view."

70. Identify one of the four stages of grief.

71. Alternatives are various _____ the client can choose in order to achieve his desired goal.

72. Establishing rapport requires that the counselor have empathy, respect and _____ for the client.

73. Name one reason why a client may come to a counselor.

74. Seeing, hearing, feeling or tasting something that does not exist is called a/an _____ .

75. Name one of the five psychological stages that many dying persons pass through before they die.

76. Name the most important thing you have to give a dying person?

77. Name one of the conflicts which Erickson claims must be resolved in adulthood and old age. _____ vs. _____ .

78. Name one of the nine steps in counseling according to the nine step model.

79. _____ is a counselor response in which the counselor points out the inconsistancies of client behavior or verbalizations.

80. Questioning is a term which is the same as the counseling response called _____ .

Part IV The following questions are short essay questions. Answer both questions on the space provided on your answer sheet.

81. Has this training course influenced the way in which you understand and communicate with people? Explain your answer.

82. In what way did this book and training course stress the belief that all humans should be treated with respect and viewed as free beings?

5

COUNSELING THE OLDER ADULT

Final Examination Answer Sheet

Part I Write **T** or **F**

1. _____

2. _____

3. _____

4. _____

5. _____

6. _____

7. _____

8. _____

9. _____

10. _____

11. _____

12. _____

13. _____

14. _____

15. _____

16. _____

17. _____

18. _____

19. _____

20. _____

21. _____

22. _____

23. _____

24. _____

25. _____

26. _____

27. _____

28. _____

29. _____

30. _____

31. _____

32. _____

33. _____

34. _____

35. _____

36. _____

37. _____

38. _____

39. _____

40. _____

41. _____

42. _____

43. _____

44. _____

Part II. Multiple Choice. Indicate your response with a letter which corresponds to your answer.

45. _____

46. _____

47. _____

48. _____

49. _____

50. _____

51. _____

52. _____

53. _____

54. _____

55. _____

56. _____

57. _____

58. _____

59. _____

60. _____

Part III. Fill in the blanks. Write a response for each statement.

61. _____

62. _____

63. _____

64. _____

65. _____

66. _____

67. _____

68. _____

69. _____

70. _____

71. _____

72. _____

73. _____

74. _____

75. _____

76. _____

77. _____

78. _____

79. _____

80. _____

PART IV. Short Essay.

81.

82.

COUNSELING THE OLDER ADULT

Instructors Answer Sheet to the Final Examination

Part I. True or False: (two credits for each correct answer).

1. T		23. F	
2. T		24. T	
3. F		25. F	
4. T		26. F	
5. T		27. T	
6. F		28. T	
7. T		29. F	
8. T		30. T	
9. T		31. F	
10. T		32. T	
11. F		33. F	
12. T		34. F	
13. T		35. F	
14. T		36. T	
15. F		37. T	
16. T		38. T	
17. T		39. F	
18. F		40. F	
19. T		41. F	
20. F		42. T	
21. F		43. F	
22. T		44. T	

Part II. Multiple Choice. (Two credits for each correct answer.)

45.	E	53.	E
46.	D	54.	C
47.	A	55.	C
48.	D	56.	C
49.	B	57.	C
50.	C	58.	D
51.	D	59.	A
52.	C	60.	E

Part III. Fill in the blanks. (Two credits for each correct answer.)

61. a) Counselee will feel understood b) supports counselee c) helps focus on feelings d) counselor can check out his hunches e) counselor conveys that he accepts client's feelings.

62. self-disclosure

63. interpretation

64. acute

65. delusion

66. depression

67. A theme in a counseling situation is an idea, feeling, attitude or belief which occurs so often in sessions that the counselor can infer that the theme is an integral part of the client's world-view.

68. It is a response that is respectful of the client and also encompasses the client's world view. a) responds to stated feelings and notes undercurrents implicit in client's statements b) appropriately emphasizes the intensity of client's feelings c) responds to non-verbal cues.

69. A person's world-view includes how he feels about himself, others, and various events which make up his life experience. This includes his belief system as well as attitudes and values.

70. shock & denial, anger, sadness, resolution

71. choices

72. concern

73. to solve a personal problem, to get help making an important decision, because they are unhappy, to learn how to handle a difficult situation, to receive help, comfort, and support during a crisis, to converse with an understanding person, to learn more about themselves.

74. hallucination

75. denial and isolation, anger, bargaining, depression, acceptance.

76. your deepest, authentic presence, genuiness

77. intimacy vs. isolation, generativity vs. stagnation, integrity vs. despair.

78. understanding the client, establishing rapport, defining the problem, setting a goal, clarifying issues, listing alternatives, exploring alternatives, supporting decisions, providing closure.

79. confrontation

80. probing

Part IV. Short Essay. (Ten credits for each answer.)